Oral Arguments and Decision Making
on the United States Supreme Court

SUNY series in American Constitutionalism
Robert J. Spitzer, editor

Oral Arguments and Decision Making on the United States Supreme Court

TIMOTHY R. JOHNSON

STATE UNIVERSITY OF NEW YORK PRESS

Cover photo: Franz Jantzen, Collection of the Supreme Court of the United States.

Published by
State University of New York Press, Albany

For information, contact State University of New York Press, Albany, NY
www.sunypress.edu

Production by Judith Block
Marketing by Susan Petrie

Library of Congress Cataloging-in-Publication Data

Johnson, Timothy Russell.
    Oral arguments and decision making on the United States Supreme Court /
Timothy R. Johnson
        p. cm. — (SUNY series in American Constitutionalism)
    Includes bibliographical references and index.
        ISBN 978-0-7914-6103-7 (hbk. : alk paper) 978-0-7914-6104-4 (pbk.)
        1. United States. Supreme Court—Rules and practice.   2. Forensic orations—
United States.   3. Judgments—United States.   4. Judicial process—United
States.   I. Title.   II. Series.

KF8742.J64 2004
347.73'2651—dc22

                                                                2003059535

10 9 8 7 6 5 4 3 2 1

For Julie, Alexi, and Aidan

Contents

Tables

Acknowledgments

Numerous people have contributed to my thinking about this book, and have challenged me to make logical, cogent arguments about how I should think about the role of oral arguments in the Supreme Court's decision-making process. Without the input of these friends, colleagues, and mentors, I would not have arrived at this final product. I note, however, that all of the remaining mistakes throughout are mine, and mine alone.

While a graduate student, I benefited from the expertise and guidance of Lee Epstein, Valerie Hoekstra, Bill Lowry, John Sprague, and Bob Salisbury. Additionally, my thinking was sparked, enhanced, and helped by conversations with Paul Djupe, Scott Comparato, Beth Wilner, Christina Wolbrecht, Andrew Martin, Brady Baybeck, John Ginkel, Scott McClurg, and Kevin Quinn. Further, most of the chapters were presented at various political science conferences and seminars over the past several years. During these meetings, I benefited from comments and criticisms from Larry Baum, Gregory Caldeira, Jerry Goldman, Susan Brodie Haire, Sunita Parikh, William McLauchlan, Lyn Mather, Michael Giles, Thomas Walker, Jeff Segal, Harold Spaeth, Rich Pacelle, Steve Wasby, and the participants of the Conference on Scientific Study of Judicial Politics at Emory University in 1997. Throughout this process I also received excellent advice from Jim Spriggs, Paul Wahlbeck, David Kimball, Laura Arnold, Paul Goren, John Freeman, Joanne Miller, and Jamie Druckman. I also appreciate the methodological advice that I received from Jim Spriggs, Paul Wahlbeck, David Kimball, Jamie Druckman, and Paul Goren. Additionally, I note the support, advice, and personal friendship of Professors Ron Christenson and Chris Gilbert at Gustavus Adolphus College. Without their guidance I would never have endeavored to become a political scientist.

I benefited from the research assistance of graduate students at Washington University, Southern Illinois University, and the University of Minnesota.

At Washington University I thank John Ginkel and Chris Hasselman for participating in intercoder reliability analysis. At SIU I had assistance from Chris Owens, Patrick Hennes, and Maria Skolarikou. At Minnesota I received assistance from Matthew Roberts, Jason Roberts, Dion Farganis, and Dan Carden.

I thank the National Science Foundation for partially funding this research through grant SBR-9709927, which allowed me to travel to Washington and Lee University, the site of Justice Lewis Powell's archives, and to the Library of Congress to analyze the papers of Justices Brennan and Douglas. I also acknowledge the financial support of the Department of Political Science at the University of Minnesota, through the MacMillan travel fund, for supporting additional research trips to these archives. During my trips to these archives, I could not have completed my research without the help of John Jacob at Washington and Lee and the librarians in the manuscript room of the Library of Congress. I am especially grateful to John Jacob for ensuring that I found, with ease, all of the data I needed from Justice Powell's oral argument notes.

At SUNY Press, Michael Rinella, Judith Block, and Robert Spitzer helped shepherd this project, and made sure that it was kept on track. I am grateful for their support.

Much of the material used throughout this book originated in other places. The crux of the manuscript comes from my doctoral dissertation written at Washington University in St. Louis. The main difference between this book and my dissertation is the inclusion of a large amount of new data, including the *amicus curiae* data used in chapters 2, 4, and 5. Additionally, the data and analysis in chapter 3 are brand new in this manuscript, as are the data and analysis in the second half of chapter 5. The vast majority of anecdotal accounts, used to illustrate the quantitative findings, are also new to this manuscript. Portions of chapter 2 and chapter 5 appear in Johnson (2001). The second half of chapter 5 was presented at the 2001 annual meeting of the Midwest Political Science Association in Chicago. Additionally, portions of chapters 2, 4, and 5 were presented at the 1999 annual meeting of the Midwest Political Science Association in Chicago, and the 1997 Conference on the Scientific Study of Judicial Politics annual meeting in Atlanta.

Finally, I would be remiss if I did not recognize my wife, Julie Maynard-Johnson, and my sons Alexi Matthew and Aidan Marshall. Julie, like many spouses, put me through graduate school with her financial and emotional support, and now endures as I continue to conduct research and write about the subjects that I love. Sometimes I am not the easiest person to live with, but she is always encouraging, supportive, and loving. As for Alexi and Aidan, they continue to keep me sane (although near the brink sometimes) and make my life outside of the academy pure joy.

Chapter 1

Introduction

In 1816, the state legislature of New Hampshire took control of Dartmouth College and acted as its new board of trustees because the college was in financial disarray. Dartmouth viewed the takeover as a political move by the newly empowered Democratic-Republicans (Smith 1989, 14), and sued the state. At the outset, the case looked dim for the college. However, after losing at trial, Daniel Webster joined Dartmouth's counsel (Jeremiah Mason and Jeremiah Smith) and argued the case on initial appeal. They lost there, too, as the Exeter Court upheld the trial court's decision allowing the state government to continue its oversight of the college (Smith 1989, 14).

Webster (a graduate of Dartmouth) filed an appeal to the Supreme Court, and in 1819 argued *Dartmouth College v. Woodward*. During oral arguments, Webster addressed the justices and argued that New Hampshire's decision to take over the Dartmouth board of trustees was made in error. He explained that a 1769 royal English charter established the college as a private educational institution and denied the state's argument that it was a public institution simply because it served the citizens of New Hampshire. Instead, citing common law, natural law, and historical records, Webster argued that state intervention was a violation of the contract clause of the U.S. Constitution.

After exhausting applicable legal reasoning, Webster laid out the policy consequences of a decision against Dartmouth College: if the Court ruled for New Hampshire, then all private institutions, not just colleges, would be in danger of losing control to the state. Specifically, Webster insisted, "It will be a dangerous experiment, to hold these institutions subject to the rise and fall of popular parties and the fluctuations of public opinions" (McIntyre 1903, in Peterson 1987, 100).

Finally, after four hours of intricate legal reasoning Webster paused and, while no exact transcript exists, O'Brien (2000) reports his final impassioned

1

plea for the justices to save the college: "Sir I know not how others feel, but for myself, when I see my Alma Mater surrounded like Caesar in the senate house, by those who are reiterating stab upon stab, I would not for this right hand, have her turn to me, and say *Et tu quoque mi fili!* And thou too, my son!" Several justices, and almost everyone in the gallery, were brought to tears and, as O'Brien notes, "Webster's oratory won the day, as it often did" (257).

This account is indicative of the early era of the Supreme Court—when great orators such as Webster, John Calhoun, and Henry Clay appeared before the Court. During this period, oral arguments were elaborate oratories but, more important, they often provided the justices with their only source of information about a case: briefs were rarely if ever submitted and outside parties did not submit *amicus curiae* (friend of the Court) briefs.

In contrast, the modern Court obtains information from many sources: litigant briefs (Epstein and Kobylka 1992), briefs *amicus curiae* (Spriggs and Wahlbeck 1997), briefs on *certiorari* (Caldeira and Wright 1988), the media (Epstein and Knight 1998a), and lower court opinions. One may wonder, then, why the Court continues to hear oral arguments when it can readily obtain an abundance of information about a case from any number of credible sources.

The answer, which I address in this monograph, is that almost all the information justices receive is what other actors want them to consider. In short, the Court has little control over the majority of information it obtains. Unless justices ask for reargument (Hoekstra and Johnson 2003) or for the parties or interest groups to file briefs that address specific issues, there is only one time for them to gather information for themselves: the oral arguments. As such, my general thesis is that *Supreme Court justices use oral arguments as an information-gathering tool to help them make substantive legal and policy decisions as close as possible to their preferred outcomes.*[1]

While this conjecture seems intuitive at first blush, many students of the Court think otherwise. Indeed, the dominant view among Court scholars is that oral arguments have little influence over case outcomes because justices' voting preferences are stable and exogenous (Segal and Spaeth 1993, 2002). As such, so the argument goes, an hour of debate about the legal and policy merits of a case will not change a justice's likely vote.

Attitudinalists are the strongest adherents of the view that oral arguments have no effect on justices' votes. As Rohde and Spaeth (1976, 153) posit, "oral argument frequently provides an indication of which is the most likely basis for decision," but it "does not . . . provide reliable clues as to how a given justice may vote." Segal and Spaeth (2002) concur with this assessment and suggest that ascertaining "The extent to which it affects the justices' votes is problematic" (280). Additionally, they contend there is no indication oral argument "regularly, or even infrequently, determines who wins and who loses"

(280). For attitudinalists, then, the short time allotted for oral arguments, combined with the fact that justices' preferences are fixed, means that their votes will not change as a result of what transpires during these proceedings.[2]

The contention that oral arguments do not affect the Court's decisions is not unique to adherents of the attitudinal model, however. For instance, Abraham (1993) points out that while questions asked during oral arguments may "forecast the ultimate decision of the Court . . . in few, if any, instances is it possible to give accurate prognosis" (193). Further, Smith (1993) suggests that the justices use these proceedings simply to "probe the attorneys' minds for additional arguments and justifications to make their case opinions more complete and compelling" (271). The bottom line is that most Court scholars still adhere to the view that the oral arguments are little more than window dressing and have no effect on how justices make decisions.[3] For them, the short time allotted for oral arguments, combined with the fact that justices' preferences are fixed, means that their votes will not change as a result of what transpires during these proceedings.[4] In short, many Court scholars simply dismiss oral arguments because they find no direct link between these proceedings and the disposition (final vote) of a case.

I do not dispute the notion that an individual justice's votes may not change based on what transpires during oral arguments, but it is naive to assume that this is the only mechanism by which these proceedings might play a role in how Supreme Court justices make decisions. Indeed, the link between oral arguments and the Court's opinions may have less to do with the disposition of cases and more to do with its substantive legal and policy decisions. In other words, while it may be difficult to draw connections between a justice's vote to affirm or reverse, the relationship between what transpires during oral arguments and the legal decisions the Court makes may be the place to uncover the influence of these proceedings.

This argument follows directly from the findings of several seminal works on Supreme Court decision making. Epstein and Kobylka (1992, 302) demonstrate that "the law and legal arguments grounded in law matter, and they matter dearly," while Maltzman, Spriggs, and Wahlbeck (2000, 5) note that "to understand fully the political dynamics of the Court, we need to move beyond a study of voting alignments to explore the multiple strategies that produce Court opinions." Thus, while oral arguments may not affect dispositive outcomes for the Court, these proceedings may very well affect the Court's substantive decisions by providing legal and policy information to the justices (Cohen 1978; Benoit 1989; Wasby, D'Amatos and Metnailer 1976). If this is the case, then scholars must reevaluate the role that oral arguments play in the Supreme Court's decision-making process. In this book I do just that by focusing on three key questions:

1. What information do Supreme Court justices obtain from oral arguments?

2. What role does the information justices gather during oral arguments play in the Court's decision-making process?

3. Under what conditions are oral arguments likely to play a role in the Court's decisions?

To answer these questions, I adopt the strategic theory of decision making, which has three tenets (Epstein and Knight 1998a). First, justices are goal oriented (with policy typically their primary objective). Second, justices' decisions depend on the choices of other actors. Third, justices' choices are affected by the institutional setting within which they work. The key is that if justices are to make efficacious decisions, while at the same time satisfying their own policy goals, they need information about each tenet of this model. While many sources provide such information to the justices, my premise is that oral arguments offer a unique means by which justices can elicit this information in cases they hear.

This research represents a key departure from extant literature on Supreme Court decision making because, to date, students of the Court have either ignored the role of oral arguments in this process or have suggested that these proceedings play little role in how justices make decisions (Segal and Spaeth 1993, 2002; Smith 1993).[5] Indeed, while scholars have studied almost every other aspect of the Court's decision-making process—from the decision to grant *certiorari* (Caldeira, Wright, and Zorn 1999) and conference discussions (Johnson, Spriggs, and Wahlbeck 2002) to the opinion-writing stage (Maltzman, Spriggs, and Wahlbeck 2002) and the final decisions on the merits (Segal and Spaeth 1993, 2002)—few have explored the one public aspect of this process. Using both qualitative and quantitative data, I demonstrate that scholars must reassess the conventional understanding of oral arguments and, in so doing, I also hope to provide further insight into our more general understanding of decision making on the U.S. Supreme Court.

The Strategic Model of Decision Making

The theoretical foundation for my account of how oral arguments help Supreme Court justices make decisions is grounded in the idea that justices are strategic actors (Cameron 1993; Epstein and Knight 1998a; Eskridge 1991a, 1991b; Ferejohn and Weingast 1992; Gely and Spiller 1990), which means that their decisions are constrained by a host of factors (Maltzman, Spriggs, and Wahlbeck

2000). Specifically, when making decisions, policy-oriented justices must account for the preferences of their immediate colleagues, the preferences of actors beyond the Court, and institutional norms and rules that might affect the decisions that they can make. This section considers the three prongs of this model.

Justices Are Goal Oriented

An abundance of evidence exists to suggest that Supreme Court justices may have many different goals (see e.g., Levi 1949; Cushman 1929; Baum 1997; Hensley, Smith, and Baugh 1997; Epstein and Knight 1998a). For example, it has been well documented that some justices seek principled decisions, or decisions that will sustain the Court's legitimacy (Baum 1997; Johnson 1996; Epstein, Segal, and Johnson 1996). While I agree that justices may have many goals, and have even argued elsewhere that justices might want to achieve goals beyond legal policy outcomes (Johnson 1995b, 1996), I follow the conventional wisdom in the study of judicial politics, which suggests that the *main goal of most Supreme Court justices is the attainment of policy in line with their personal preferences* (Segal and Spaeth 1993, 2002; Maltzman, Spriggs, and Wahlbeck 2000). As Epstein and Knight (1998a, 8) point out, "[J]ustices, first and foremost, wish to see their policy preferences etched into law."

That policy is the main goal of Supreme Court justices is neither a new nor a controversial idea. Rather, this argument is well grounded in the work of legal realists such as Llewellyn (1931) and Frank (1949) and early judicial behavior scholars such as Pritchett (1948), Murphy (1964), and Schubert (1965). Scholars have provided empirical support for this argument in several ways—three of which I address here. First, individual justices' voting patterns are quite consistent over time. For instance, with the exception of two terms (1974 and 1977), Lewis Powell voted liberally in civil liberties cases no more than 43 percent of the time in any given term. Likewise, William Brennan's liberal support for civil liberties fell below 70 percent during only one term of his Court tenure (1969) (Epstein et al. 1996, 456). This consistency indicates that justices pursue specific policy goals and rarely waver from doing so.

Beyond voting patterns, Epstein and Knight (1998a, 30–32) demonstrate that almost 50 percent of all remarks made by justices during the Court's conference discussions concern policy, and 65 percent of statements in circulating memoranda during the opinion-writing process address policy considerations. These remarks include statements about legal principles the Court should adopt, courses of action the Court should take, or a justice's beliefs about the content of public policy. *Seattle Times Co. v. Rhinehart* (1984) illustrates this point. In this case a religious organization (the Aquarian Foundation) sued the

Seattle Times for defamation and invasion of its members' privacy. The specific dispute surrounded the foundation's allegation that the newspaper knowingly printed fictitious stories about the organization's practices and members. During pretrial discovery, a controversy arose when the trial judge issued an order compelling Rhinehart (and his group) to provide the *Seattle Times* with a list of donors and members, and simultaneously imposed a protective order prohibiting the paper from publishing these names.[6] The paper argued that the protective order violated its First Amendment right to publish the names, and it focused on this issue in its appeal to the Supreme Court.

During the opinion-writing stage of this case, Justice Brennan wrote a memo to Justice Powell about Powell's interpretation of the existing discovery rules under the *Federal Rules of Civil Procedure*. Brennan wrote, "Although it is undoubtedly true that discovery proceedings 'are not public components of a civil trial,' I am not sure that the materials generated by discovery are not, as a matter of modern practice, open to the public" (memo to Powell, May 3, 1984). In short, and in accordance with Epstein and Knight's argument, Brennan pointed out how he believed the policy should be interpreted and therefore how the Court should rule.

Finally, scholars address the interactions that take place between justices (Maltzman, Spriggs, and Wahlbeck 2000; Epstein and Knight 1998a; Murphy 1964). They point to justices' bargaining statements during the opinion-writing phase of a case to demonstrate that policy considerations are the driving force behind justices' decisions. In *Rhinehart,* Brennan's memo to Powell also included a statement of this nature. Indeed, he begins the memo as follows: "Thank you for your note of May 1, and for your consideration of my suggestions. If you could find your way to incorporating them I would be pleased to join your opinion" (memo to Powell, May 3, 1984). Of course, some of these memos are more forceful, but the point is the same—to move the policy set by the Court closer to a particular outcome.

Justices Are Strategic

The attitudinal model of Supreme Court decision making argues that justices are unconstrained in their ability to vote for their most preferred policy outcomes because they enjoy life tenure (Segal and Spaeth 1993, 2002). In other words, because justices do not face election or retention, and because they usually do not have higher political ambitions, they can vote for their most preferred outcomes without consequence. In contrast, the strategic model suggests that, although they pursue policy goals, justices cannot always make decisions that conform perfectly to their preferences. Rather, because five justices must usually agree on a decision to set precedent, and because external institutions (such as Congress) can sanction the Court, justices must pay particular attention to the preferences and likely actions of their immediate colleagues as well as those beyond the marble palace. In short, Supreme Court justices alter their behavior in order to achieve their goals within the context of the political environment. In this section, I separately consider intra-Court strategic interaction and interinstitutional strategic interaction.

INTRA-COURT STRATEGIC INTERACTIONS. A recent, yet rich, literature explores the extent and impact of internal bargaining between justices (see e.g., Johnson, Spriggs, and Wahlbeck 2002; Maltzman, Spriggs, and Wahlbeck 2000; Caldeira, Wright, and Zorn 1999; Epstein and Knight 1998a; Schwartz 1997). These works are progeny of Murphy (1964), who argued that justices are rational actors and act as such when deciding cases. The reason for this is obvious, as Murphy notes: "Since he shares decision making authority with eight other judges, the first problem that a policy oriented justice would confront is that of obtaining at least four, and hopefully eight, additional votes for the results he wants and the kinds of opinions he thinks should be written in cases important to his objectives" (37).

While Murphy did not systematically test his theory, others have done so. For example, in an analysis of the private papers of Justice Brennan and Justice Marshall, Epstein and Knight (1995) demonstrate that over 50 percent of cases in one sample contained one or more bargaining statements between the justices.[7] In a later monograph, Epstein and Knight (1996a, 18)conclude that "law, as it is generated by the Supreme Court, is the result of short-term strategic interactions among the justices and between the Court and other branches of government."

Wahlbeck, Spriggs, and Maltzman (1998) support these findings in their empirical analysis of opinion circulation on the Court. They find that an opinion goes through more drafts as the ideological heterogeneity of a majority coalition increases, as the number of suggestions given to the opinion writer by other justices increases, as the number of threats made to the opinion writer increases, and as the number of times other justices say they are yet unable to join an opinion increases. This suggests to Wahlbeck, Spriggs, and Maltzman that "Opinion authors' actions are shaped by the interplay of their own policy preferences and the actions of their colleagues" (312).

Wahlbeck, Maltzman, and Spriggs (1996) find evidence that the decision to join a majority opinion is a strategic choice as well. Specifically, they demonstrate that the decision to join is determined by how acceptable a majority opinion is to a specific justice, whether that justice can obtain concessions from the opinion writer, and the past relationship between the opinion writer and the justice deciding whether to join. Finally, Maltzman, Spriggs, and Wahlbeck (2000) provide evidence that how the chief justice assigns opinions, how justices respond to initial opinion drafts, and how coalitions form are all processes grounded in strategic interaction.[8] This means that the process through which the Court makes decisions is a product of interactions and interdependencies between the justices. If, on the other hand, justices simply voted for their most preferred outcomes, there would be no evidence of bargaining and accommodation behind the scenes of the decision-making process.

INTERINSTITUTIONAL STRATEGIC INTERACTION. The ability of Supreme Court justices to reach their most preferred outcomes is not only constrained by their immediate colleagues' preferences. Other scholars have shown that justices must be aware of political forces beyond the Court and take these forces into consideration during their decision-making process (Marks 1989; Gely and Spiller 1990; Eskridge 1991a, 1991b; Ferejohn and Weingast 1992; Cameron 1993; Martin 1997; Johnson 2003). Justices must do so to prevent other institutions (e.g., Congress and the executive branch) from sanctioning the Court for making decisions with which they disagree. To avoid these sanctions, existing accounts suggest that justices think about whether their actions will provoke such reactions.

   Consider the Court's relationship with Congress. Scholars who study the impact of the separation of powers note that the justices do not stray too far, too often, from how Congress wants them to act because a congressional majority can override statutory decisions with which it disagrees.[9] Intuitively, an override is most likely to happen when the Court and Congress are ideologically incompatible, which means that the justices will rule consistently with Congress if the median member of the House and the filibuster pivot in the Senate (Krehbiel 1998) are both ideologically opposed to the median justice's preferred outcome. Indeed, if the Court rules against the policy preferences of the pivotal members in this situation, Congress would have the necessary votes to pass a law overriding the decision (Eskridge 1991a). Such a scenario took place when the Court used *Employment Division, Department of Human Resources of Oregon v. Smith* (1990) to overturn *Sherbert v. Verner* (1963), which, until that point, limited regulation of religious practices without a compelling governmental interest. Congress subsequently overturned *Smith* with the 1993 Religious Freedom Restoration Act (RFRA) and ultimately codified the compelling interest test set out in *Sherbert* (Epstein and Walker 1998b).[10]

   Clearly, Congress has the authority to overturn Court decisions, and it has done so. However, if the two houses of Congress are divided over an issue, then the justices are free to place decisions anywhere within the ideological boundaries of the two houses (Wolbrecht 1994). Wolbrecht notes that the justices found themselves in this situation when they decided the free exercise cases of *Braunfeld v. Brown* (1961) and *Sherbert v. Verner* (1963).[11] There are also times when the Senate and the House of Representatives are aligned, but cannot garner enough votes to overrule a Court decision. In this scenario, the justices can place policy wherever they choose (Eskridge 1991b). Eskridge (1991a) argues that the justices were in this position when the Court reversed a series of civil rights cases during the 1989 term, which implicated Title VII of the Civil Rights Act of 1964. While Congress tried to overturn these decisions with the Civil Rights Act of 1990, the bill failed to pass.

The justices must also be cognizant of how the executive branch will react to their decisions because the president can sanction the Court in a number of ways if he, or an executive agency, does not agree with the decisions.[12] First, although executive agencies have the power to enforce the Court's decisions, they do not have to do so. As Epstein and Walker (1998a, 43) note, "The bureaucracy can assist the Court in implementing its policies, or it can hinder the Court by refusing to do so, a fact of which the justices are well aware." While scholars debate about whether the president fully controls the bureaucracy, and is able to use it for his political advantage, Moe (1982) demonstrates that presidents have some control over independent commissions. Thus, even though a president may not be able to unilaterally order an agency to disregard a Court decision, the threat of an agency shirking Supreme Court decisions is real and has been carried out in the past. Wasby (1993, 330) notes that the Reagan administration had a policy of "nonacquiescence" for lower court judicial decisions that it disliked, especially in Social Security cases.

While the president may not have total control over the bureaucracy, he can personally sanction the Court by refusing to enforce its decisions. The most oft-cited example of this behavior is President Jackson's response to a Court decision that he particularly disliked: "John Marshall has made his decision, now let him enforce it" (Ducat 1996, 110). Other confrontations demonstrate that the president can, and does, judge whether the Court has made the right decision. For instance, President Jackson vetoed a bill that established a national bank, even after the Court declared such an entity constitutional (Wasby 1993). Several years later President Lincoln defied the Taney Court by refusing to release an alleged traitor, imprisoned while the right of *habeas corpus* was suspended, even though the Court ordered him to do so (Wasby 1993). This concern about enforcement is not relegated to the nineteenth century. Rather, Ducat (1996, 110) notes Justice Frankfurter's concern when the Court decided *Brown v. Board of Education* (1955): "Nothing could be worse from my point of view than for this Court to make an abstract declaration that segregation is bad and then have it evaded by tricks."

Beyond refusing enforcement, the administration can support anti-Court action in Congress if the president or an agency disagrees with the justices' policy choices (Baum 1995a, 159). Two examples illustrate this tactic: President Roosevelt's Court-packing plan in response to the justices' continued rejection of his administration's New Deal policies, and President Jefferson's involvement in forwarding the impeachment of Justice Samuel Chase (Rehnquist 1992, 22–23). Finally, presidents and their advisors can publicly criticize the Court if they disagree with its decisions (Baum 1995a, 159), or they can fail to support it for decisions with which they disagree. Baum (1995a) argues that President Reagan and his Justice Department often used the former strategy, while President Eisenhower used the latter tactic.

In general, while rarely invoked by the executive branch, the sanctions delineated here may decrease the Court's power as the ultimate arbiter of the law. It is easy to see why. If an administration refuses to enforce the justices' decisions, then the Court is impotent to make or affect policy. Similarly, public criticism or anti-Court measures can erode the Court's legitimacy. Thus, Supreme Court justices must account for how the executive branch may react to their decisions, and ensure that they do not stray too far, too often, from its preferred policy goals. In other words, justices "act strategically, anticipating the wishes of the executive branch, and responding accordingly to avoid a confrontation." (Epstein and Walker 1998a, 43).

Justices Account for Institutional Rules

The final tenet of the strategic model suggests that, although justices are goal oriented and consider other actors' preferences when making decisions, they must also account for the institutional context within which they decide cases (Slotnick 1978; Danelski 1978; Maltzman and Wahlbeck 1996b; Epstein, Segal, and Johnson 1996). By institutions, I mean the rules (either formal or informal) that structure interactions between social actors (Knight 1992). In the context of the Court, legal institutions may constrain a justice's ability to make certain decisions. That is, the "rules of the game" may prevent the justices from always making decisions that equate with their most preferred outcomes. The reason for this is simple: Supreme Court justices comply with institutional rules and norms (like precedent) because the Court must at least have the aura of acting as a legal, nonpolitical, institution (Hoekstra and Johnson 1996; Epstein and Knight 1998a).

For instance, Knight and Epstein (1996) argue that justices adhere to the norm of respecting precedent. While their findings are far from general (they only analyze thirteen cases), the evidence is nonetheless compelling. Indeed, if respect for precedent were not a norm, then Knight and Epstein would not have found evidence that the justices frequently discuss past cases in their private deliberations. Such references often take the form of Justice White's memo to Justice Powell in *Gertz v. Robert Welch Inc.* (1974)—one of the Court's most famous libel cases. White wrote:

> I would leave unprotected by the First Amendment, along with obscenity, fighting words, and other speech that is sufficiently violence prone [he cites *Beauharnais* 1952, *Chaplinsky* 1942, and *Cantwell* 1940]. As was the case in *Metromedia* (1971), I am unaware of any satisfactory evidence or basis for further restricting state court power to protect private persons against reputation-damaging falsehoods published by the press or others. (memo from White to Powell, January 10, 1974)

That the justices make such references to precedents in private memos suggests that they act as if they themselves are constrained to follow these decisions. The question, however, is, why do the justices feel constrained by precedent? For Knight and Epstein (1996, 1029) the answer is simple: "compliance with this norm is necessary to maintain the fundamental legitimacy of the Supreme Court." In other words, they argue that if the Court frequently ignored its own legal precedents, its credibility as a judicial institution might be questioned, and it could potentially lose legitimacy—its main source of power.

Respecting precedent is an informal norm, but the Court must also follow certain formal rules such as those set out in the Constitution. Because the Constitution gives Congress the power to override Supreme Court decisions, the justices must account for the preferences of Congress when deciding where to set policy in a particular area of law. Other codified rules are found in Article III of the Constitution; these include the Court's jurisdiction to hear certain cases,[13] the requirement that a party must have standing (*Flast v. Cohen* 1968) to be heard in the Supreme Court, and that a case must be justiciable before the Court will consider ruling on it.[14]

The Court's "Biased" Information Problem

The theory outlined above establishes that Supreme Court justices are strategic actors whose primary goal is to see the law reflect their personal policy preferences. However, to make laws that are both efficacious and in line with their preferred policy goals, justices need information that will help them assess how each tenet of the strategic model may affect the decisions they can make. That is, justices need information about the policy options available to them, how their immediate colleagues want to decide a case, how other actors such as Congress, the president, and the public may react to a decision, and whether institutional norms or rules might limit their ability to make a particular decision. Without such information, it would be virtually impossible for the justices to make decisions that satisfy, as closely as possible, their own policy preferences. As such, it is no surprise that they seek, and receive, information from a variety of sources.

The two most pervasive sources of information for the Court are litigant and *amicus curiae* briefs (Caldeira and Wright 1988; Epstein and Kobylka 1992; Epstein 1993; Spriggs and Wahlbeck 1997; Epstein and Knight 1998b). Briefs submitted by the parties alone often account for hundreds of pages of legal arguments. Consider Supreme Court Rule 33.1, which sets the page requirements for all briefs filed to the Court (from the *certiorari* stage to the final decision stage).[15] Parties who petition the Court to hear their case can submit up to a thirty-page brief, and those opposing this motion have thirty pages to respond. During the *certiorari* stage the parties can also submit supplemental briefs of up to ten pages in length. If the petition for *cert.* is granted, then the attorneys submit briefs on the merits—up to fifty pages in length—to explain why the Court should rule in favor of their client.[16] Finally, *amici curiae* can submit twenty-page briefs at the *cert.* stage and thirty-page briefs on the merits.[17] Legal briefs are not the justices' only source of information, however. They also have access to every lower court decision related to a case, their own precedents in the same issue area, law review articles, and media accounts of the controversy.

This abundance of information decreases the "information problem" facing the justices (Caldeira and Wright 1988). Indeed, at each stage of their decision-making process the justices gather information about a wide range of policy options, how external actors might react to their decisions, and what institutions might limit their choices. But, while the general information problem may be solved, the justices face another potential problem: almost all of the information provided by litigants, *amici*, or other sources (law reviews, lower court decisions, etc.) is what *others* want the justices to see and have. For instance, if the Catholic League for Religious Liberties and the National Association for Women submit briefs *amicus curiae* in an abortion case, each is certain to argue that the Court should rule in a manner consistent with its membership's policy goals—either to overturn *Roe v. Wade* (1973), or to increase the freedom of women to choose abortion as an option during pregnancy. This is an important point because it suggests that almost all of the information in the Court's possession invariably reflects the goals and preferences of the parties who present it to the Court. I designate this phenomenon the Court's "biased information problem."

Ultimately, if the justices make decisions based solely on information that others provide to the Court, several adverse consequences might result. First, litigant and *amicus* briefs (for example) may not provide a path by which the justices can reach a decision at or near their most preferred policy choices.[18] Second, unless the justices obtain information about how external actors may react to a particular decision, they may have a more difficult time creating efficacious and lasting policies (Martin 1996, 1997; Eskridge 1991a). For example, as noted in the previous section, Congress might sanction the Court if the justices often decide cases out of line with the preferences of the pivotal member. Finally, the litigant briefs, *amicus* briefs, or lower court decisions may fail to adequately elucidate institutional constraints the Court may face as a case winds its way from the *certiorari* stage to a final decision on the merits.

Solving the Biased Information Problem: The Role of Oral Arguments

While scholars have studied the kinds of information actors provide to the Court (Epstein and Kobylka 1992; Spriggs and Wahlbeck 1997), and while others have focused on the Court's "lack of information" problem (Caldeira and Wright 1988), none have analyzed the effect of the biased information that justices do receive from external sources. I do so by analyzing how the justices can overcome the biased information problem as they procure information on their own terms during oral arguments. These proceedings often afford the justices their only chance to obtain information that they want, and often need, in a much less biased form.[19] Indeed, during oral arguments a justice can probe the litigants about issues that may help her reach an efficacious decision that is also near her preferred policy.[20] Scholarly accounts as well as the justices themselves suggest that this is the case.

Evidence from the Academy

Existing anecdotal evidence suggests that Supreme Court justices use information garnered from oral arguments when writing opinions. For instance, in a comparison of justices' inquiries during oral arguments with positions taken by the majority in *Tennessee Valley Authority v. Hill* (1978), Cohen (1978) finds explicit instances where Justices Powell and Stevens utilized issues discussed during the oral arguments in their opinions.[21] More recently, Benoit (1989) analyzes four incorporation cases to discern whether the Court's majority opinions include issues advanced by the winning party during oral arguments. Benoit's findings corroborate Cohen's but also make a key improvement over the earlier work, because his method controls for issues raised during oral arguments that were not discussed in the litigants' briefs, as well as for those that were raised in both instances. This is important, because Benoit's findings suggest that oral arguments may provide unique information to the Court beyond the litigants' briefed arguments.

Wasby, D'Amato, and Metrailer (1976) find instances where the Court relied on oral arguments across a series of school desegregation cases. The analysis leads them to conclude that justices use oral arguments for several functions. First, the main role of these proceedings is to provide information that allows justices "to obtain support for their own positions or to assure themselves with respect to an eventual outcome" (418). Second, Wasby and his colleagues claim oral arguments help the justices gain a sense of how their colleagues view a case. Third, they argue that justices use this time to inquire about the beliefs of external actors such as the legislative and executive branches (419). These findings suggest that justices may use oral arguments as a strategic information-gathering tool. Unfortunately, the hypotheses are only tested on an analysis of cases within one issue area—desegregation.

Beyond the anecdotal accounts, two systematic accounts of oral arguments exist in the literature. Schubert et al. (1992) employ a biosocial approach to analyze how the Court utilizes oral arguments. They find that these proceedings provide a time for justices to clarify the issues of a case and to persuade their colleagues about these issues. This approach has merit, but Schubert et al. do not specifically focus on the types of information the justices gather; rather they are interested in how the justices act during these proceedings. Additionally, Wasby et al. (1992) demonstrate that "The Court's *per curiam* opinions provide clear evidence that oral argument at times—but certainly not always—has been directly relevant to the Court's disposition of a case—and at times determinative of outcome" (30). Although Wasby et al. use a nonrandom sample, their analysis suggests even more clearly that oral arguments play an informational role in how the Court makes decisions, at least those that are *per curiam*.[22]

Perspectives from the Bench

Almost universally, past and present justices publicly agree with the scholarly assessments concerning oral arguments. While there is some dissension from this view, Justice Robert Jackson (1951) summed up the general sentiment: "I think the justices would answer unanimously that now, as traditionally, they rely heavily on oral presentations . . . it always is of the highest, and often of controlling, importance." (801). Justice Lewis F. Powell reaffirmed Jackson's sentiment several decades later: "the fact is, as every judge knows . . . the oral argument . . . does contribute significantly to the development of precedents" (in Stern, Gressman, and Shapiro 1993, 571). Other justices posit that these proceedings do, at times, have a great effect on their decisions (see e.g., Hughes 1928; White 1982; Rehnquist 2001). If past and present Supreme Court justices maintain that oral arguments provide information that helps them decide cases, then the notion that the information obtained during these proceedings might influence the Court's decisions gains additional merit. This section considers not only these general statements, but also the more specific claims about how the justices think oral arguments affect their decisions.

Former Chief Justice Hughes (1928, 61) wrote that, in most cases, the impressions a justice develops during oral arguments "accord with the conviction which controls his final vote." While a justice may enter oral arguments with relatively clear preferences concerning the outcome of a case (as the attitudinal model assumes), the arguments can mitigate or crystallize these preferences. To support this claim, Hughes (1928, 62) explains that one of his colleagues from the New York Court of Appeals kept track of his immediate post–oral argument impressions of a case, and that 90 percent of the time these thoughts accorded with his final vote.

This account resembles Justice Harlan's experience with oral arguments at the Court. When he kept a diary of his postargument impressions of a case, Harlan (1955, 7) found that "more times than not, the views which I had at the end of the day's session jibed with the final views I formed after the more careful study of the briefs." Contemporary justices support the conclusions drawn by Justices Hughes and Harlan. For instance, Justice Brennan asserts that "I have had too many occasions when my judgment of a decision has turned on what happened in oral argument" (in Stern, Gressman, and Shapiro 1993, 732). He goes on to suggest that, while not controlling his votes, this process helps form his substantive thoughts about a case: "Often my idea of how a case shapes up is changed by oral argument" (in Stern,Gressman, and Shapiro 1993, 732).

These insights raise the possibility that oral arguments can force justices to reassess their perceptions about the substantive issues involved in cases they hear. This, then, may lead to changes—not necessarily of votes—but of the policy choices made within a written opinion. Chief Justice Rehnquist (2001) agrees with this assertion and argues that oral advocacy can affect his thoughts about specific cases: "I think that in a significant minority of cases in which I have heard oral argument, I have left the bench feeling different about the case than I did when I came on the bench. The change is seldom a full one-hundred-and-eighty-degree swing" (243).

The notion that oral arguments can affect substantive decisions is widely accepted by many Supreme Court justices. However, not all members of the bench were initially convinced that this process was even remotely important. Justice Antonin Scalia, for one, thought that oral arguments were "a dog and pony show" before joining the bench, but after serving almost a decade on the Court he came to believe that "Things can be put in perspective during oral argument in a way that they can't in a written brief" (in O'Brien 2000, 260). Chief Justice Rehnquist (2001) confirms this point and argues that a good oral argument "will have something to do with how the case comes out" (244).

Clearly, these public statements suggest that justices believe oral arguments play a key role in how they decide cases, but why? Different justices provide different answers to this question. Chief Justice Rehnquist (1984) posits that oral arguments allow justices to evaluate counsel's "strong and weak points, and to ask . . . some questions [about the case]" (1025). Similarly, Justice Byron White (1982, 383) suggests that during these proceedings the Court treats lawyers as resources. By this, he seems to suggest that counsel come to the Court to provide new or clarifying information, which enables the justices to gain a clearer picture of the case at hand. Indeed, there may be points about which the justices are still unclear after reading the briefs, and this face-to-face exchange can make them clearer. As Chief Justice Rehnquist (2001, 245) argues: "One can do his level best to digest from the briefs . . . what he believes necessary to decide the case, and still find himself falling short in one aspect or another of either the law or the facts. Oral argument can cure these shortcomings."

Justice William O. Douglas holds a somewhat different perspective on oral arguments. He argues that these proceedings are meant to teach the justices about the key points of a case: "The purpose of a hearing is that the Court may learn what it does not know . . . It is the education of the Justices . . . that is the essential function of the appellate lawyer" (in Galloway 1989, 84). Moreover, Justice John Harlan (1955) claims oral arguments are the best mechanism for information gathering: "there is no substitute . . . for the Socratic method of procedure in getting at the real heart of an issue and in finding out where the truth lies" (7).

That oral arguments provide the justices with an opportunity to query the litigants and gather information is intuitive. While the briefs may address almost every legal intricacy, counsel cannot always know what information the justices want. It is only during oral arguments, then, that justices can discuss the issues that pique their interests. As Chief Justice Rehnquist (1984, 1021) writes: "Oral argument offers a direct interchange of ideas between court and counsel . . . Counsel can play a significant role in responding to the concerns of the judges, concerns that counsel won't always be able to anticipate when preparing briefs." Thus, for him, oral argument is "Probably the most important catalyst for generating further thought" (Rehnquist 2001, 241).[23]

Rehnquist (1986) best sums up how justices perceive oral arguments: "Justices of the Supreme Court of the United States have almost unanimously agreed that effective oral advocacy is one of the most powerful tools of the professions" (289). Even the principal skeptic (Justice Scalia) changed his view once he joined the Court.

The justices' accounts reinforce the existing empirical findings and provide compelling support for the idea that, in certain instances, oral arguments play a key role in how the justices make decisions. The works of Benoit (1989), Cohen (1978), and Miller and Barron (1975) demonstrate that relationships exist between orally argued issues and positions used by the justices in their opinions. Additionally, the implication of Wasby, D'Amato, and Metrailer's (1976) analysis is that oral arguments help the justices make decisions that are close to their preferred policy goals, and help them account for the preferences of other actors (both on and beyond the Court). Combined with the justices' public statements, these works demonstrate that a systematic analysis of the informational role oral arguments play in the Supreme Court's decision-making process is warranted. This is my task in this book.

Studying Oral Arguments Systematically

Theoretically, a systematic examination of oral arguments has not been conducted because many scholars argue that we can understand Supreme Court decision making without accounting for these proceedings. Practically, such an analysis is seemingly unfeasible because the data are very difficult to obtain. Indeed, while the Court makes oral argument transcripts available to the public, it does so only on microfiche and reel-to-reel tapes.[24] Moreover, the written transcripts are often more than fifty pages long per case, and they do not delineate which justices ask which questions during the proceedings. Instead, they identify the questioner as simply "the Court."[25] As a result, scholars have largely relied on case studies or journalistic accounts (e.g., Galloway 1989; Lane 2000) to determine the role oral arguments might play in the Court's decision-making process.

To test my hypothesis that oral arguments are a strategic, information-gathering tool for the Court, I rely on several sources of original data: litigant and *amicus* briefs, oral argument transcripts, notes and memoranda from the private papers of Supreme Court justices, and the final decisions handed down by the Court. I gather these data for a sample of cases decided between 1972 and 1986.

First, I utilize the briefs submitted by the parties as well as by all *amici curiae* involved in a case. I do so because the briefs often set the initial policy and legal boundaries for cases heard by the Court (see Lawrence 1990; Epstein and Kobylka 1992; Wahlbeck 1998). Second, I analyze the corresponding oral argument transcripts for each case to determine which issues pique the justices' interest during oral arguments. Instead of focusing on issues raised by the attorneys, note that I focus only on questions raised by the Court, because I am interested in the types of information the justices want, rather than what information the attorneys want them to have. This allows me to ascertain whether, consistent with my general hypothesis, justices use oral arguments to gather information about their policy options, other actors' preferences, and institutional constraints they may face.[26]

Third, I rely on the private papers of Justices Brennan and Douglas, located at the Library of Congress, and those of Justice Powell, located at Washington and Lee University Law School in Lexington, Virginia. I analyze these justices' conference notes and intra-Court memoranda to discern when, and how often, the justices discuss issues raised at oral arguments during conference and when opinions are circulated between chambers. Fourth, to determine the extent to which the justices use oral arguments to learn about their colleagues' perceptions of a case, I utilize the notes Justice Powell took during oral arguments. I do so because, within these notes, Powell kept track of questions raised and comments made by his colleagues. Fifth, I compare the questions raised during oral arguments with the major issues decided in majority opinions.

Finally, I utilize data beyond my sample from Spaeth's *Expanded Supreme Court Database* (2001) and his *Burger Court Database* (2001) obtained from the Inter-University Consortium for Political and Social Research. These data sets contain information from the Vinson, Warren, and Burger Courts about all aspects of Supreme Court decision making—from the decision on *certiorari*, to conference votes, to the final votes on the merits. Combined with an analysis of all formally decided cases during this period, I am able to conduct a final test of the strategic use of oral arguments. That is, I use the Spaeth data to determine the circumstances under which the Supreme Court turns to oral arguments when making substantive decisions.

My task is to use these data to systematically explain the role oral arguments play in the Supreme Court's decision-making process. Only by comparing the oral argument transcripts with the justice's internal records and final opinions can I test whether information from these proceedings plays a strategic and informational role for the Supreme Court. By analyzing the sample of cases from the Burger Court, as well as the cases drawn from Spaeth databases, I am able to argue that my findings are generalizable beyond a few cases.

Chapter Outline

The book follows the course that a case takes from the filing of briefs, to oral arguments, through conference and the opinion-writing stage, and finally to the Court's decisions on the merits. Chapter 2 begins with an exploration of the information justices have prior to oral arguments—from the litigant and *amicus* briefs. From there it explores the types of information (policy considerations, external actors' preferences, etc.) that justices seek to gather during oral arguments. Chapter 3 draws on game-theoretic cheap talk literature (Gibbons 1992; Morrow 1994; Farrell 1987; Crawford and Sobel 1982) to argue that justices also use oral arguments to learn about their colleagues' perceptions of a case, and who they may have to persuade to procure a majority coalition during and after conference.

Chapter 4 looks at when, and to what extent, justices invoke information from the oral arguments in their conference discussions and in memoranda sent to the Court during the opinion-writing stage. I am particularly interested in how often justices invoke any information from these proceedings, and more important, how often they discuss issues raised for the first time during the oral arguments, as opposed to information that originated in the litigant or *amici curiae* briefs. This is a key advance over previous work because, to date, scholars have not yet analyzed the extent to which the justices discuss oral arguments in their private deliberations.

Chapter 5 takes the final step by exploring the extent to which information from the oral arguments finds its way into the Court's majority opinions. Additionally, this chapter provides a systematic explanation of the circumstances under which we should expect the Court to turn to oral arguments in its opinions.

In the concluding chapter, I tie together the theory and empirical analysis. Specifically, I summarize the role oral arguments play for the Supreme Court, and what impact these proceedings have on the justices' decision-making process. This chapter also clarifies where the findings of each chapter fit into the overall framework of judicial decision making, how they may help us understand other branches of government, their implications for future studies of decision making, and their implications for our notion of the Court's countermajoritarian role in our system of democracy.

Chapter 2

———◆◈◆———

Oral Arguments as an
Information-Gathering Tool

Introduction

During the initial oral arguments in *Roe v. Wade* (1973), Justice White questioned Sarah Weddington (counsel for Roe) about an issue not addressed by either of the parties in their briefs.[1] He was concerned with whether or not abortions could be performed on demand throughout a pregnancy, or whether the state had an interest in restricting abortions at some point during the forty-week term. To determine the answer to this query, Justice White asked: "And the statute does not make any distinction based upon at what period of pregnancy the abortion was performed?" Weddington's response was unambiguous: "No, Your Honor. There is no limit or indication of time, whatsoever" (transcript of oral argument, 18–19). While he did not pursue the issue, it was clear that Justice White could not comprehend how women could possess the same constitutional right to have an abortion on demand immediately prior to birth and shortly after conception.

During the next term, when the Court heard rearguments in *Roe,* the question of when (if ever) a state's interest in protecting an unborn fetus outweighs a woman's interest in obtaining an abortion on demand was a focal point—only this time Justice White asked for more detail from Weddington.[2] One exchange, in particular, highlights his concern:

JUSTICE WHITE: Well, I gather your argument is that a state may not protect the life of the fetus or prevent an abortion even at any time during pregnancy?

MRS. WEDDINGTON: At this—

21

JUSTICE WHITE: Right up until the moment of birth?

MRS. WEDDINGTON: At this time my point is that this particular statute is unconstitutional.

JUSTICE WHITE: I understand that. But your argument, the way you state it is that it wouldn't make any difference when in the pregnancy that the State attempts to prevent the abortion? It would still be unconstitutional?

MRS. WEDDINGTON: At this time there is no indication to show that the Constitution would give any protection prior to birth. That is not before the Court. And that is the question that

JUSTICE WHITE: Well, I don't know whether it is or it isn't. If the statute—you're claiming that the statute is void on its face?

MRS. WEDDINGTON: That's correct.

JUSTICE WHITE: Now isn't it possible, if the statute—before you can declare the statute void on its face, that you have to say that it's void no matter when in the pregnancy the abortion takes place?

MRS. WEDDINGTON: It seems to me in this situation the Court is— excuse me. I must—would you ask the question again?

JUSTICE WHITE: Well, is the statute void—would the statute be void on its face if the State could prevent abortions at any time after six months?

MRS. WEDDINGTON: You mean if the State, in fact, did that?

JUSTICE WHITE: Well, let's assume it were constitutional for the State to prevent abortions after six months.

MRS. WEDDINGTON: It would still be void on its face in this situation because it's overly broad. It interferes at a time when a state has no

JUSTICE WHITE: Well, this isn't a free speech case. The statute might be perfectly valid in part, and invalid in part. You're saying it's invalid on its face—totally invalid—that it may not apply to—the statute may not prevent an abortion, no matter when the abortion takes place.

MRS. WEDDINGTON: My argument would first be that it's void on its face. And, second, if the Court finds it's not void on its face, it certainly is void because it infringes upon the fundamental right at a time when the State can show no compelling interest early in pregnancy. (transcript of oral argument, 43–45)

The argument between Justice White and Sarah Weddington highlights two key points. First, during oral arguments the justices raise specific policy issues (defined as questions about legal principles the Court should adopt, courses of action the Court should take, or a justice's beliefs about the content of public policy) about a case. In this instance, Justice White focused on limits the Court should set on a woman's right to choose an abortion on demand. Even though he ultimately dissented in *Roe,* this inquiry alluded to the Court's eventual answer: a state and a woman both have interests, and the emphasis on whose interest is preeminent changes over the course of a pregnancy.

Second, the White/Weddington exchange implies that justices use oral arguments to raise issues not broached by the litigants or *amici curiae* in their legal briefs submitted to the Court. Indeed, the issue of when a state's interest in regulating abortions becomes compelling was only briefed because the Court asked the parties to do so prior to reargument and, as the above exchange indicates, Weddington did not even think the issue was before the Court.[3] Consistent with my theory outlined in chapter 1, then, Justice White used the oral arguments in *Roe* as an information-gathering tool; he raised a policy issue (on which the Court's decision turned), and introduced an issue that was not part of the record prior to the original oral arguments.

Strategy, Information, and Oral Arguments

The strategic account outlined in chapter 1, existing anecdotal evidence, and justices' own experiences suggest that oral arguments have the potential to play a key informational role in the Court's decision-making process. The sheer number of questions raised by the justices during these proceedings supports this assumption. Indeed, in the sample used for this study, the justices asked an average of 88 questions per case (SD = 29.09) or, during a typical one-hour oral argument, 1.5 questions per minute.[4] This leads to the general hypothesis I test in this chapter:

> **Information-Gathering Hypothesis: Supreme Court justices use oral arguments as an information gathering tool to help them make decisions as close as possible to their preferred goals.**

More specifically, this hypothesis encompasses four types of information I expect justices to focus on during oral arguments. In this section, I outline these types and the corresponding hypotheses.

Policy Considerations

The first tenet of the strategic account is that justices strive to achieve their most preferred policy objectives. To do so, they need information about all the policy choices available to them. I posit that oral arguments provide a time for justices to gather this information by raising questions concerning legal principles the Court should adopt, courses of action the Court should take, or a justice's beliefs about the content of public policy. These types of questions can help the justices clarify the policy choices presented to them, as well as to determine whether choices exist beyond those presented by the parties and *amici curiae*. Consider, for example, the oral arguments in *Hunt v. McNair* (1973), where the Court was asked to determine the constitutionality of the South Carolina Educational Facilities Authority Act (SCEFAA). The SCEFAA authorized financing, through the issuance of revenue bonds, for a Baptist college. In assessing the constitutionality of this law, one justice used the oral arguments to determine what Hunt's counsel wanted the Court to do: "Now, you are here asking us to invalidate the statute? Would you throw the whole statute out" (transcript of oral argument, 9)?

The justices may also use oral arguments to flesh out the content of existing policies and how they should be interpreted. In *Martin v. Ohio* (1987), the Court sought to determine whether the burden of proof shifts from the state to the defendant in a murder case when the defendant claims the killing was an act of self-defense. While many of the Court's questions addressed this issue, one particular exchange exemplified the justices' willingness to address policy concerns.

COURT: Counsel, this jury is instructed to acquit unless the state proves beyond a reasonable doubt that there was this intentional purposeful killing.

COUNSEL: Correct.

COURT: But then the jury is told that this self-defense must be proved beyond—by a preponderance of the evidence. Why shouldn't the instruction be to the jury, that the defendant proves a claim of self-defense? And if its evidence about self-defense raises a reasonable doubt whether the defendant killed purposefully, you should acquit? Doesn't it really water down the reasonable doubt standard to say that before there is reasonable doubt raised by the defendant's evidence with respect to self defense, which goes to purposefulness, he has got to prove it beyond a—by a preponderance of the evidence? (transcript of oral argument, 33)

Consistent with Wasby, D'Amato, and Metrailer (1976), these cases demonstrate that justices raise questions about policy issues during oral arguments. Combined with existing literature that suggests making good legal policy is the preeminent concern of justices (Pritchett 1948; Murphy 1964; Epstein and Knight 1998a; Maltzman, Spriggs, and Wahlbeck 2000), I hypothesize the following:

Information Hypothesis 1: During oral arguments the most prevalent questions from the bench should examine policy concerns about a case.

Examination of External Actors' Preferences

Because actors beyond the Court may sanction the justices for decisions with which they disagree, I also expect the justices to raise a significant number of questions about external actors' preferences and their possible reactions to the Court's decisions.[5] Most generally, justices can ask straightforward questions about positions held by Congress, the president, the bureaucracy, or the public.

Consider an example from *Immigration and Naturalization Service v. Chadha* (1983), where the justices dealt with the constitutionality of the legislative veto in the context of an INS decision to deport an alien who possessed an expired visa. During oral arguments, the Court was concerned with the preferences of both the executive and legislative branches. Justice O'Connor inquired about Congress's historical power in this area: "May I inquire also whether historically the Congress has used its sovereign power over aliens to enact specific legislation to deport specific individuals" (transcript of oral argument, 15)?[6] Another justice asked counsel about the role of the executive branch: "How does the executive get into the process at the stage of Resolution 926" (transcript of oral argument, 25)?

Beyond questions about actors' explicit preferences, justices can also gather information about other actors by questioning the litigants about the breadth and impact of the Court's decisions as well as by asking hypothetical questions (Prettyman 1984; Baum 1995b; Wasby 1993; Smith 1993). They may ask such questions to determine how broadly those who implement the Court's decisions may construe its legal and policy dictates, and whether the Court is likely to incur negative reactions from those who make these implementation choices. Prettyman (1984) highlights the use of hypothetical questions in *Board of Education v. Pico* (1982) to demonstrate this point. This case focused on whether a public school board could remove books from school libraries that it considered morally, socially, or politically objectionable. During the arguments, the Court asked two pertinent questions. One justice asked: "Would you say that it would be appropriate to remove all books in the library that contained any disparaging remarks about blacks or Jews?" (Prettyman 1984, 557). Another posited, "If the board chose to remove books containing favorable references to Republicans because it was a good Democratic board, we should not let that go on to be examined?" (Prettyman 1984, 557). These questions suggest that the justices wanted to examine exactly how broadly school boards throughout the country might construe a decision that favored book removal. This is consistent with how they use hypothetical questions more generally. As Biskupic (2000, A17) notes, "The justices say such questions [hypotheticals] help them figure out the consequences of a case, how their ruling could affect other situations down the line." The key point is that the justices want other actors to comply with their decisions and to construe them correctly, so they ask questions, including hypotheticals, to help them make these determinations.

Overall, because the Court relies on others to enforce, comply with, and uphold its decisions, the justices ask questions about the preferences and possible reactions of boards of education, the public, and Congress. They also test the limits of their decisions by raising hypothetical questions as well as questions about the possible impact of their decisions. Thus, I expect the following:

Information Hypothesis 2: Justices should use oral arguments to gather information about the preferences of actors beyond the Court, and about the impact of their decisions, at about the same rate as they gather information about policy issues.

Examination of Institutional Constraints

The third tenet of the strategic model posits that the Supreme Court is constrained by a number of institutional rules. As such, I also expect the justices to address these issues during oral arguments in an effort to determine how these rules might affect the decisions they make. However, I do not expect them to raise questions about institutions at the same rate as they address policy concerns and external actors' preferences. The reason stems from the Court's own rules and from its jurisdiction as outlined in Article III, Section 2 of the Constitution. First, Court rules specify that all parties must include jurisdictional statements in their briefs (both for *certiorari* and on the merits).[7] Second, each brief on the merits must include a list of precedents, statutes, and constitutional provisions applicable to the case.[8] Finally, the Constitution mandates that the Court can only decide cases and controversies under the law.[9] Given these rules, and the fact that the parties want to ensure that a case and controversy exists, the briefs submitted prior to oral arguments almost always address these issues in an in-depth manner. Only in rare instances where the briefs do not do so, or when circumstances change (e.g., a case becomes moot after the Court accepts it for review), do I expect the Court to raise these types of issues during oral arguments.[10]

Even though I do not expect justices to ask many questions about institutional norms and rules, I still expect some focus on these issues because institutional rules can inhibit a justice's ability to reach a particular outcome in a case. For instance, a justice may use oral arguments to probe the applicability and interpretation of relevant precedent. In *Lemon v. Kurtzman* (1973), the Court was asked to determine the constitutionality of using tax monies to reimburse nonpublic schools for expenses such as teacher salaries, books, and instructional materials (Epstein and Walker 1998b, 163). During oral arguments, one justice inquired about the applicability of the standard set in *Walz v. Tax Commission of the City of New York* (1970): "At least some of the opinions in *Walz* suggest that there might be a distinction between subsidy situations and tax exemptions? Isn't it fair to say that the Court's opinion indicated some doubt—at least doubt—about direct subsidy" (transcript of oral argument, 37)?

Along with raising questions about informal norms, I expect Supreme Court justices to ask the parties about formal rules—such as jurisdiction and justiciability—so they can ensure a case is properly before the Court. In *Hortonville Joint School District No. 1 v. Hortonville Education Association* (1976), the Court considered whether a school board could terminate teachers for striking without first providing a hearing before an impartial decision maker. During oral arguments, Justice White asked whether a federal question even existed in the case:

> It seems to me what you ought to be arguing is to dismiss this case on the ground it has not any federal question in it. You keep talking about Wisconsin law. As I understood, we brought the case here because there was a federal issue in it. The Wisconsin Supreme Court decided that the school board wasn't an unbiased body to make any decision at all. And that is the issue that is here. Why should we be arguing about what Wisconsin law means?

More recently, in *Bush v. Gore* (2000), Justices Kennedy and O'Connor queried whether a federal question existed in the disputed Florida election. Immediately upon beginning his oral arguments, Justice Kennedy asked Theodore Olson (Bush's attorney): "Can you begin by telling us our federal jurisdiction, where is the federal question here" (transcript of oral argument, 1)?

These examples demonstrate that the justices do raise questions about institutional rules. However, I do not expect them to focus on these issues as often as they focus on policy and external actors' preferences. This leads me to hypothesize the following:

Information Hypothesis 3: Justices should raise questions about formal and informal institutional constraints during oral arguments, but less frequently than they raise questions about policy and external actors' preferences.

Expansion of the Written Record

The first three hypotheses focus on the explicit nature of information I expect justices to garner from oral arguments. My final hypothesis more directly addresses the biased information problem. Based on the assumption that most of the information the Court possesses prior to oral arguments is biased in favor of those who provide it, these proceedings give the justices an opportunity to place new issues on the record that the parties and *amici* do not address.[11] They can do so by asking questions similar to those posed by Justice White in *Roe*. Additionally, consider a question posed in *Heller v. New York* (1973). In this case, the Court was asked to decide whether prisoners have the right to formal parole hearings. Because the litigant briefs did not explain what they meant by a "formal hearing," a justice raised this question during oral arguments: "Your concept of an adversary hearing then would be where the counsel for the defendant would have a right to cross-examine the magistrate" (transcript of oral argument, 13)?

Although they do not test whether the Court generally raises questions like the one posed in Heller, Wasby, D'Amato, and Metrailer (1976) find that justices use oral arguments to raise questions "outside the boundaries established by the parties' arguments" (414). Wasby and several other colleagues (1992, 7) argue that "Oral argument may also lead the Court to decide that issues should be added [to the record]." Given the biased information problem, combined with the anecdotal findings from these previous studies, I expect the following:

Information Hypothesis 4: Justices should utilize oral arguments to raise issues that were not presented in the litigant or *amicus* briefs.

More specifically, I expect justices to be significantly more concerned with adding issues to the record than with clarifying issues already on it. Indeed, if justices are strategic actors who want information that will help them reach their preferred outcomes, then there is no reason to expect them to discuss only the arguments already provided in written briefs.

Data and Coding Schemes

To begin explaining the informational role oral arguments play for the Supreme Court, I need evidence regarding which issues set the initial boundaries in a case, as well as which issues are actually raised by the justices during these proceedings. To obtain this evidence, I drew a random sample of seventy-five cases argued between 1972 and 1986 from Spaeth's *Supreme Court Database* (2003).[12] For each case I compared the issues raised in the briefs (litigant and *amicus*) with the questions raised by the justices in the oral argument transcripts. This comparison allows me to test the above hypotheses by determining the types of information the justices are most interested in obtaining during the oral arguments, and whether they mainly address briefed issues or raise questions about issues not already on the record. This section explains the data collection and coding procedures used for this analysis.

Litigant Briefs

Before I can make any claims about whether oral arguments provide information to the justices, I need a baseline upon which to determine what issues have the potential to be discussed during these proceedings. Existing research demonstrates that the legal briefs submitted to the Court often set the boundaries of a case by framing the issues for the justices (Wahlbeck 1998; Johnson 1996; Epstein and Kobylka 1992; Lawrence 1990). Following the logic of these studies, I obtained the briefs submitted by all parties and *amici curiae* involved in each of the seventy-five cases in the sample, and coded every argument that they raised. This yielded a sample of 385 arguments in cases when no *amici* participated and a sample of 505 arguments when *amicus* briefs were submitted.[13]

The choice of coding rules and procedures used to determine what issues are raised in the written briefs is a difficult one, and there is significant disagreement in the literature concerning this process. McGuire and Palmer (1995, 1996) argue that the most objective procedure is to code the questions posed in the "Questions Presented" section of the litigant briefs for each case.[14] In contrast, Epstein, Segal, and Johnson (1996) argue that a researcher should code the entire body of the brief because any issue forwarded in the body is considered a part of the record.

Spriggs and Wahlbeck (1997) provide a coding scheme that is a compromise between the McGuire/Palmer and the Epstein/Segal/Johnson approaches. Indeed, they code the issue headings located in the "Argument" section of each brief. This is an appropriate method for several reasons. First, as Spriggs and Wahlbeck (1997, 370) point out, "Supreme Court Rule 24.6 mandates that briefs be 'logically arranged with proper headings.'" This means that the major arguments should be outlined in the section headings. Second, Stern, Gressman, and Shapiro (1993, 548) argue that these headings tell the reader exactly the point that will be made in each section, which means they provide a good measure of the arguments contained in the brief. Most important, however, is that the Spriggs and Wahlbeck coding scheme is efficient (the coder does not have to read the minutia of a brief to determine the arguments being made), rigorous (it focuses on specific arguments rather than generalities), and objective (the coder need only look at the heading rather than subjectively interpret hundreds of pages of text). For these reasons, I utilize the Spriggs and Wahlbeck (1997) method of coding briefs.[15]

Written Oral Argument Transcripts

Obviously, the most important data for my purposes are drawn from the transcripts of oral arguments. I code every question asked by the Court to determine the types of issues justices raise during these proceedings as well as whether these issues originated in the briefs or were raised by the Court for the first time during oral arguments. In the cases without *amicus* participation the Court asked 3,223 questions, and in cases with *amici curiae* the justices asked 2,344 questions.[16]

Although the oral argument transcripts are a rich data source, the analysis of them is somewhat troublesome in that they do not explicitly note which justice asks which questions to the parties. Instead, the transcripts only say "Court" or "Question" before each question. This is a problem, because I cannot differentiate between the individual justices' questions and therefore cannot draw any conclusions about whether individual justices seek similar information during oral arguments.[17] Given that making inferences about individual behavior from aggregate data is untenable (see e.g., Huckfeldt and Sprague 1995; King 1997), these data only allow me to make claims about how the Court as a whole acts during oral arguments.

Despite this shortcoming, an aggregate analysis of oral arguments can still help scholars understand the role these proceedings play for the Court. Indeed, the more important an issue is to the justices, the more often the Court as a whole should raise questions about that issue. Thus, if the Court focuses most of its questions on policy, then there is evidence that the justices are generally policy oriented and use oral arguments to probe for the best means by which to obtain their preferred policy outcomes. This is an important, although not perfect, step because this is the first study to systematically determine the kinds of information that justices gain by participating in oral arguments.

Second, these data allow me to determine whether the Court as a whole raises new issues during oral arguments and, if so, what new issue types they raise most often. If the justices seek information beyond what the parties and *amici curiae* provide, then there is evidence that these proceedings play a unique informational role for the Court.

*Individual-Level Data: The Bench Notes of Lewis F. Powell and
Landmark Cases*

Assessing the informational role of oral arguments using aggregate data is clearly not an optimal situation. Thus, I augment the aggregate data by analyzing the behavior of four individual justices in a limited sample of cases. First, of all the Burger Court justices whose private notes and records are available to the public, Justice Powell kept track of issues raised during oral arguments. These notes are one of the richest data sources for understanding what information justices seek during oral arguments, and they allow me to construct a profile of issues that Powell found important during these proceedings.[18] Doing so allows me to compare the information Powell sought with the information sought by the Court as a whole. If the results are similar, then the aggregate findings gain additional weight.

Second, using *Landmark Briefs and Arguments of the Supreme Court of the United States* (Kurland and Casper 1975), I analyze the oral argument behavior of three other justices. In these volumes Kurland and Casper combine litigant briefs, *amicus* briefs, and the oral argument transcripts in major cases to give the reader a sense of exactly what arguments were presented to the Court. In a number of cases, the editors list which justices ask which questions during oral arguments, as opposed to just listing "Court" or "Question" as in the official transcripts. Combining these data with the Powell notes allows me to make individual claims (albeit only on a limited basis) to help corroborate the aggregate findings based on the larger sample of cases.

There are three important caveats about the *Landmark Briefs*. First, between 1964 and 1989 Kurland and Casper named specific justices in only eight cases.[19] This presents two key problems. First, all of these cases are from outside of the time frame of my sample. This means that I may not be able to accurately compare behavior of justices because the dynamic of oral arguments may have changed between the Warren Court and the Burger Court. Additionally, only three of the justices in these eight cases were on the bench for the entire period of my sample.[20] As a result, for purposes of comparison, I analyze the behavior of only four justices (including Powell).[21]

The second caveat is that the *Landmark Briefs* comprise a small sample. Indeed, as I use only seven of the cases represented, I may not be able to make general claims about these justices' behavior. However, even with only a few cases I can look for trends that support the aggregate findings. Finally, because all of these cases are considered landmark decisions, I may also encounter problems of generalizability. That is, some scholars (Baum 1995b) argue that the justices act differently during oral arguments in highly salient cases (like *Roe*) than they do in everyday cases (e.g., tax cases, antitrust cases).

In the end, while there are shortcomings to both the Powell and the *Landmark Briefs* data, they allow me to initially test the validity of the aggregate analysis.

Coding Scheme

Because I am interested in the kinds of information justices possess when making decisions, I created a general coding scheme to capture all arguments that may materialize in a case; it includes six finite categories.[22] Using these categories, I code every major argument offered in the litigant and *amicus* briefs, and every question raised by the Court during oral arguments. This allows me to determine the types of information provided to the justices prior to the oral arguments and, more important, the types of information they seek during these proceedings. This section explains the six categories that make up the coding scheme.

First, *constitutional* issues are arguments concerning applicable clauses or amendments to the Constitution. Focus on these types of issues provides evidence that the justices are concerned with legal issues surrounding a case.[23] As such, I am able to compare the prevalence of legal arguments versus policy arguments in the Court's decision-making process. While there are many ways to measure the Court's focus on the law, a focus on constitutional issues allows me to explicitly distinguish these arguments from policy issues.

Second, *policy* issues are those arguments that focus on legal principles the Court should adopt, courses of action the Court should take, or a justice's beliefs about the content of public policy (see Epstein and Knight 1998a).

The third category includes all issues that may help the justices determine the preferences or possible reactions of *external actors*. These include arguments that explicitly refer to external actors' preferences, the implications of a case, and hypothetical questions asked by the Court during oral arguments. Each of these subsets provides information about the external ramifications of a case for the justices. First, obtaining information about other actors' preferences allows the justices to assess how close to their own preferred outcome they can place policy without incurring sanctions from actors whose preferred outcomes may differ from the Court's. Second, issues concerning the implications of a case tell the justices who will likely be affected by their decisions, and to what extent they will be affected. Third, hypothetical questions help the Court determine how broadly actors beyond the Court will interpret a particular decision. As Prettyman (1984) notes, these questions help the Court test "the outer reaches . . . of what the Court may in fact have to decide" (556).

Thus, these questions help the justices determine how other actors might interpret and implement specific policy choices.

The final three categories are self-explanatory. *Factual issues* include any references to case facts, the record, or evidence. *Precedent* includes arguments that invoke prior cases decided by the Court.[24] Finally, *threshold issues* are defined as arguments about jurisdictional or justiciability concerns. These categories, explicated in table 2.1, cover the range of issues that could arise in a case.[25] Using them, I content analyze the litigant briefs, *amicus* briefs, and the oral argument transcripts to determine which issues the Court addresses during these proceedings.

To show more clearly how these issue categories are used in the analysis throughout this chapter (and the remainder of the book), table 2.2 provides an overview of each issue type. The first column lists the hypothesized focus of the Court, the second column lists the coding category used to test for the Court's interest in each issue type, and the last two columns provide examples of these issues from the briefs and from the Court's oral argument questions.

Table 2.1
Issue Types Used to Code Litigant Briefs, *Amicus* Briefs, and Oral Argument Transcripts

1. Constitutional Issues	Any mention of the Constitution, in a context such as "Law X violates the First Amendment."
2. Policy	Questions about legal principles the Court should adopt, courses of action the Court should take, or a justice's beliefs about the content of public policy.
3. External Actor's Preferences	Any references to the preferences of an external actor (including but not limited to: Congress, an agency, a state, the public, and lower courts). Additionally, any references to a lower court's policy choice, the standards used by a lower court, the implications of a decision, and all hypothetical questions posed by the Court.
4. Facts	Specific mention of facts of the case, any mention of the record, and questions of evidence.
5. Precedent	Statements invoking previously decided cases, references to specific cases, or statements such as "In previous cases the Court held . . ."
6. Threshold Issues	Any mention of jurisdiction or justiciability (e.g., standing, mootness, ripeness).

Table 2.2
Issue Areas Supporting Hypothesized Court Focus

Issue Area	Supporting Issue Type	Briefs	Oral Arguments
Policy	Questions about legal principles the Court should take, courses of action the Court should take, or a justice's beliefs about the content of public policy	An appellate Court performing its duty of independently determining the issue of obscenity must view the materials as obscene (*Marks v. U.S.*).	Is the purpose of the community standard to draw on the frame of reference that the juror normally looks to, such as the district from which the venire is drawn; or is it to look at the market—the economic market in which the challenged film is exhibited? Which is the more relevant (*Marks v. U.S.*)?
External Actors	External actors' preferences, hypothetical questions, and the implications of a case	Congress has repeatedly rejected similar arguments subsequent to the enactment of the Freedom of Information Act (*U.S. v. Weber Aircraft Corp.*).	Do you think that courts generally have given the statutory language in Section 5 its literal meaning, or has there been some indication, not only in this Court, in others, that we have to be careful about applying it as it appears to be written (*U.S. v. Weber Aircraft Corp.*)?
Precedent	Precedent	The Florida right of reply statute is entirely consistent with the major premise of *New York Times v. Sullivan* (*Miami Herald v. Tornillo*).	Well, do I misread him as having suggested that under our decision in *Winship* every element of the criminal offense to be proved by the [reasonable doubt standard] (*McKinney v. Alabama*)?

Threshold Issues	Threshold barriers	The Court has jurisdiction to hear this case (*Miami Herald v. Tornillo*).	Before the North Dakota case, do you think you might have had some serious troubles on jurisdiction here (*Miami Herald v. Tornillo*)?
Legal Arguments	Constitutional provisions	The requirement that servicemen obtain the approval of the base commander before distributing petitions on base does not violate the First Amendment (*Brown v. Glines*).	The only remaining question is whether the ban violates the constitution (*Brown v. Glines*)?
Facts	Facts	The respondent in this case did not act with malice (*Gertz v. Welch*).	Counsel, did I understand you to say that in each of these clinics there was an hour-long consultation with the patient prior to the abortion (*City of Akron v. Akron Center for Reproductive Health*)?

Results

As argued in the previous section, to make claims about the types of information Supreme Court justices might gather during oral arguments, there must be a baseline to indicate what arguments have the potential to be discussed during these proceedings. Following existing research (Epstein and Kobylka 1992), the baseline I use consists of the issues raised by the parties and *amici curiae* in their briefs submitted to the Court. By examining the issues provided to the Court, I can determine the types of information that the justices possess prior to oral arguments.[26]

Table 2.3 provides a snapshot of the types of information provided to the justices in cases when *amici curiae* do not participate, as well as in cases when they do participate. Consider the top half of the table first. In these cases, the litigants focus the majority of their briefed arguments on policy and legal considerations: 40 percent of the major arguments deal with issues of policy, while 31 percent deal with constitutional issues. Given justices' policy orientation (Pritchett 1948; Segal and Spaeth 1993; Epstein and Knight 1998a), and lawyers' knowledge of this fact (McGuire 1993a, 1993b) it is intuitive why the briefs focus the plurality of arguments on these issues.[27] Additionally, because the law constrains the justices (Knight and Epstein 1996; Maltzman, Spriggs, and Wahlbeck 2000), the parties know that they must provide significant analyses of the legal (in my case constitutional) issues surrounding a case. Thus, even though policy considerations are predominant in the briefs, litigants do not stray too far from legal analysis.

Seattle Times Co. v. Rhinehart (1984) highlights litigants' use of policy and legal analysis in their briefs (see chapter 1 for the specific facts of this case). In its brief, the *Times* asserted a course of action that it wanted the justices to take: the justices should apply a test that would recognize the First Amendment interest in free press and limit the government's interest in issuing protective orders. In response, Rhinehart's attorneys argued that the current policy (Washington Civil Rule 26 (c)) adequately protected the paper's rights. In other words, the petitioner's brief asked the Court to take a specific action, and the respondent's brief provided an alternative policy—maintaining the status quo.

In *Rhinehart* the parties also provided legal (constitutional) arguments. The petitioner argued that the paper possessed substantial First Amendment rights to disseminate newsworthy information. Alternatively, Rhinehart argued that the foundation members' First Amendment rights to associational privacy and religious freedom should be the justices' paramount concern. This example demonstrates that, while the parties clearly focus on policy issues, they do not

Table 2.3
Types of Information Provided to the Supreme Court
in Litigant and *Amicus* Briefs

Cases without *Amicus* Participation (*N* = 45 Cases)[a]

Issue Area	Arguments Raised in Litigant Briefs	Percentage
Constitutional	118	31[b]
Policy	154	40
External Actors	28	7
Precedent	49	13
Threshold	20	5
Facts	16	4
Total	385	100

Cases with *Amicus* Participation (*N* = 30 Cases)[c]

Issue	Arguments Raised By			
	Litigant Brief Area Only	*Amicus* Brief Only	Litigant and *Amicus* Brief	Total
Constitutional	18 (10)	15 (9)	140 (81)	173 (34)[d]
Policy	45 (19)	28 (12)	159 (69)	232 (46)
External Actors	3 (7)	24 (53)	18 (40)	45 (9)
Precedent	9 (23)	25 (62)	6 (15)	40 (8)
Threshold	10 (77)	2 (15)	1 (8)	13 (3)
Facts	1 (50)	1 (50)	0 (0)	2 (0)
Total	86 (17)	95 (19)	324 (64)	505 (100)

a In the full sample of cases (75), 45 had no amicus participation. Therefore, the main source of information for the justices is the litigants' briefs.
b Percentages are rounded to the nearest whole number.
c Thirty cases contained at least one *amicus* brief.
d Percentages in the last column are the total percentage of each issue type raised by the litigants or *amici*.

ignore the legal components of a case. In short, attorneys arguing before the nation's highest Court know that "the law and legal arguments grounded in the law matter, and they matter dearly" (Epstein and Kobylka 1992, 302).

Rhinehart is also indicative of the general focus in litigants' briefs. Indeed, neither of the litigants specifically dealt with the preferences of external actors, precedent, the facts of the case, or threshold issues. These findings mirror the results in table 2.3, which demonstrates that only arguments about precedent receive more than 10 percent of the litigants' attention. The other categories—external actors' preferences, threshold issues, and the facts—are virtually ignored in the legal briefs.[28]

The bottom half of table 2.3 explores the types of information the Court receives from the briefs when *amici curiae* participate. Note first that, with the exception of arguments about precedent and external actors, the vast majority of information provided by *amici* reiterates arguments presented by the parties. Indeed, of all the arguments provided to the Court prior to oral arguments, 64 percent are found in both litigant and *amicus* briefs. Additionally, 69 percent of policy arguments and 81 percent of constitutional arguments fall into this category. This comports with Spriggs and Wahlbeck's (1997, 382) finding that "an *amicus curiae* brief's role most likely does not pertain to their contributing novel arguments but more likely rests with reiterating party arguments." In short, the justices may not find new arguments imbedded in *amicus* briefs, but by addressing issues already in the litigants' briefs, *amici* seem to signal the Court about what may be the most salient issues in a case.

Differences also exist in the types of information the Court receives when *amici* participate. Specifically, two points are noteworthy. When *amici* join a case, the Court receives slightly more information (although the difference is not statistically significant) from the briefs about the preferences and possible reactions of external actors. This corroborates Epstein and Knight's (1998b) argument that "organized interests—participating as *amicus curiae*—provide information about the preferences of other actors" (215). Additionally, the Court does not gain a significant amount of additional information from *amici* about relevant precedent, threshold issues, or the facts of a case. In other words, even when *amici* participate, the briefs focus the majority of their arguments on legal issues and policy concerns.

Aggregate Court Behavior during Oral Arguments

The analysis of the legal briefs provides the necessary baseline upon which to compare the issues that justices may address during oral arguments. I now consider these proceedings and reiterate the first three hypotheses. First,

I expect justices to spend the vast majority of time asking questions about policy considerations. Second, the justices should raise questions about external actors at about the same rate as they raise policy questions. Finally, while I expect the justices to focus on institutional constraints, they should ask fewer questions about threshold issues and precedent than they do about policy and external actors' preferences.

THE COURT'S FOCUS ON POLICY CHOICES. Table 2.4 demonstrates that justices are more concerned with questions of policy than with any of the other issue types. In cases without *amici* participation, 40 percent of the Court's questions focus on policy, and this increases to 43 percent when *amici* participate. Differences of means tests, which compare the number of policy questions with the number of queries about each of the other issue types, corroborate the Court's emphasis on policy. Clearly, the Court asks significantly more questions about policy than about constitutional issues, relevant precedent, or threshold issues ($p < .001$ for each relationship).[29]

What exactly does it mean for the Court to raise policy issues? The answer can be found throughout my sample of cases. Consider *Allstate Insurance Co. v. Hague* (1981). In this case, the justices were asked to decide how much Allstate should pay a widow whose husband was killed in a motorcycle accident near the Minnesota border, but in Wisconsin. Although the deceased did not have insurance for the motorcycle, he held three policies covering three other vehicles. Each policy contained an uninsured motorist clause, but limited the payout to $15,000 for each vehicle. Hague's widow, also a resident of Wisconsin at the time of the accident, subsequently gained residence in Minnesota, and argued that Minnesota law allowed her to "stack" the three policies. According to Hague, this meant that Allstate should pay her $45,000. Allstate countered that Wisconsin law should control the suit because the policy was invoked based on an accident that occurred in Wisconsin, and all those involved in the accident were residents of Wisconsin. As such, Allstate wanted Wisconsin law to apply (which did not allow the stacking of policies), so that it only had to pay the benefits from one policy.

During oral arguments, the Court focused on the choice of law doctrine, and the justices were interested in how to construe this doctrine given that the accident happened so close to the border of Minnesota. Thus, one justice inquired: "Do these distances [from the borders] make a difference in applying choice of law concepts or do lines, boundaries on maps" (transcript of oral argument, 21)? Additionally, the justices wanted to know whether the question of jurisdiction led to a clear result of which state law should apply: "But you do not think that we should say that just because a state court has jurisdiction—

Table 2.4

The Focus of the Court's Questions during Oral Arguments by Issue Area and Source of Information

Cases without *Amicus* Participation (N = 45 Cases)

Issue Area	Oral Argument Questions About		Total
	Briefed Issues	New Issue[a]	
Constitutional	142 (45)[b]	176 (55)	318 (10)***[c]
Policy	330 (25)	974 (75)***	1304 (40)
External Actors	37 (3)	1122 (97)***	1159 (36)
Precedent	82 (26)	234 (74)***	316 (10)***
Threshold	40 (32)	86 (68)***	126 (4)***
Total	631 (20)	2592 (80)***	3223 (100)

Cases with *Amicus* Participation (*N* = 30 Cases)

Issue Area	Oral Argument Questions About				
	Litigant Brief Only	*Amicus* Brief Only	Litigant and *Amicus* Brief	New Issue[a]	Total
Constitutional	18 (8)	18 (8)[b]	114 (50)	78 (34)	228 (10)[c]***
Policy	53 (5)	48 (5)	232 (23)	685 (67)***	1018 (43)
External Actors	0 (0)	10 (1)	17 (2)	760 (97)***	787 (34)
Precedent	7 (3)	24 (11)	4 (2)	181 (84)***	216 (9)***
Threshold	3 (3)	3 (3)	1 (1)	88 (93)**	95 (4)***
Total	81 (4)	103 (4)	368 (16)	1792 (76)***	2344 (100)

a New issues are operationalized as those which were not raised in the briefs submitted prior to oral arguments. The Court raises them for the first time during these proceedings.

b Percentages are in parentheses. They are calculated horizontally for each issue area.

c Percentages in the last column are calculated for each issue type raised by the Court.

Note: T-tests in the columns labeled "New Issue" are conducted to determine whether the Court's focus during oral arguments is on new issues or on issues first raised in the briefs. In the top half of the table, the test is run on the mean number of new questions versus the mean number of questions about briefed issues for each type. In the lower half of the table the tests are conducted between columns 4 and 5. T-tests are also conducted in the "Total" columns in each half of the table. The tests in this column compare the mean number of policy issues raised during oral arguments with each of the other issue areas.

* = Difference is significant at 0.10 level; ** = Difference is significant at the 0.01 level; *** = Difference is significant at the 0.001 level (two-tailed tests).

obvious jurisdiction, no one questions it—that it may apply its own law" (transcript of oral argument, 38)? In short, the Court was interested in discerning how to determine the appropriate policy choice (which state's insurance law should apply).[30]

While the justices raise questions about how to apply specific laws or policies, as in *Allstate,* they are also concerned with standards and principles by which they should decide. That is, the justices often inquire about which legal tests they should use to decide a case. Questions of this nature are exemplified in *City of Akron v. Akron Center for Reproductive Health* (1983), where the Court considered the constitutionality of the city's abortion ordinance.[31] The city's main argument was that it only needed a rational basis for its stringent abortion regulations to withstand constitutional muster.[32] At least one justice wanted the city's attorney to explain how he viewed Akron's interest in enforcing the five specific provisions of the law.

> COUNSEL: . . . if the burden is only insubstantial, all the state need show is that there is a rational basis for the legislation . . .
>
> COURT: Counsel, is the city relying on all four of the alleged state interests you described in this instance?
>
> COUNSEL: That's correct your honor. (transcript of oral argument, 7)

The justices were also interested in determining how broadly the city wanted the Court to interpret the ordinance. To this end, one justice posed the following question: "Are you asking that *Roe v. Wade* be overruled . . . It seems to me that your brief in essence asks either that, or the overruling of *Marbury against Madison*" (transcript of oral argument, 21)? In other words, the justices wanted to know the city's interest and what it wanted the Court to do about abortion policy more generally.

The oral arguments in *Turner v. Safley* (1987) provide another example of how the justices use oral arguments to determine which legal test to apply. Here the Court considered the constitutionality of regulations promulgated by the Missouri Division of Corrections. The regulation in question prohibited correspondence between inmates at different prisons unless it was deemed in the best interests of the parties (the exception was correspondence about legal matters). Further, the regulation allowed inmates to marry only if they obtained the prison superintendent's permission, and when the reason for marrying was compelling.[33] During oral arguments, one justice asked respondent counsel about which legal standard (compelling interest or rational basis) the Court should use to decide the case.

COURT: Compelling reason [for disallowing marriage] is less vague, certainly, than the conditions for allowing prison mail, which were unspecified.

COUNSEL: Yes sir. I would agree that it is vague. I do not suggest that it is—that there is a common method of understanding. We asked the various prison administrators who testified what their definition was, and they did not come down to exactly the same thing. For example, a defendant Blackwell testified that financial considerations would be good enough to allow two inmates to get married . . .

COURT: Well you might ask the nine of us what constitutes a least onerous alternative, and we might all come up with different answers to that. But it is a standard, anyway, just as compelling reason is a standard.

COUNSEL: Yes sir, it is. And I return to the proposition that I do not think that prison authorities have the power, in the absence of some compelling reason that they advance . . . to stop two consenting adults, who satisfy the statutes of MO, from getting married. (transcript of oral argument, 55)

These examples suggest that the justices are interested in understanding, and making judgments about, policies on which they will have to rule. Combined with the data from table 2.4, they support the hypothesis that during oral arguments the justices are intensely concerned with policy issues.

THE COURT'S FOCUS ON EXTERNAL ACTORS. The second information hypothesis is that justices should ask a commensurate number of questions about the preferences of actors external to the Court. Table 2.4 demonstrates that this is the case, as 1,159 (36 percent) questions fall into this category when *amici* are not present in a case. This total is similar when *amici* participate: 787 (34 percent). Additionally, differences of means tests demonstrate that, with the exception of questions about policy, the justices are significantly more likely to ask questions about external actors' preferences than about any of the other issue types ($p < .001$ for each relationship). This finding indicates that the justices know they must account for how other actors may react to the Court's decisions. More important, it indicates that the justices use oral arguments as a key source to obtain this information, given that the briefs rarely provide information about other actors' preferences (see table 2.3).

Like examples of the Court's focus on policy, there are also numerous exchanges that exemplify the justices' focus on external actors during oral arguments. First, I examine questions about legislative intent, proclamations made by Congress about existing law, and powers possessed by Congress. From there I offer several examples of how the justices use oral arguments to discuss the current administration's stance on a case, public opinion, the implications of deciding in a certain manner, and hypothetical questions.

In *Chrysler Corporation v. Brown* (1979), the Court sought to discern whether the Freedom of Information Act (FOIA) applied to documents held by a government agency, but which contained information about a private corporation. As soon as Chrysler's counsel began his argument, the questioning moved to Congress's views of the FOIA exemptions:

> COUNSEL: But as to these exemptions, Congress still made them permissive only. When I say permissive, it gave the agencies discretion to withhold those documents if it needed to, but it made clear in the legislative history that those exemptions were not to be invoked unless it was truly necessary to protect the governmental interest.
>
> COURT: Which legislative history are you talking about, the Senate or the House?
>
> COUNSEL: This comes through, in fact, in both the Senate and the House version. It comes through in the sense that, although there are statements made concerning the permissive nature of the exemption, the only time that they are made is with respect to those exemptions relating to governmental interest. In contrast, when the Congress remarked concerning Exemption 4, which was an exemption designed to protect private interests, its statements were in the sense of mandatory remarks that the exemption must be enforced and must be utilized to protect those private interests.
>
> COURT: This is committee report?
>
> COUNSEL: These are the committee reports . . . the House stated that Exemption 4 "would assure the confidentiality of confidential business information obtained by the government." And during the Senate hearings, the statement was made, "Such protection must be afforded not only as a matter of fairness but . . . as a matter of right."
>
> COURT: Well, I have always had the feeling that the House report was written by the proponents and the Senate report was written by the opponents or vice versa. I find those reports quite contradictory. (transcript of oral argument, 10)

Questions about legislative intent are important because they help the justices decipher a piece of legislation and determine how Congress might react to a particular decision. The problem with these questions is that they tell the Court about the preferences of the Congress that enacted the legislation rather than about those of the Congress currently in power. Because it is the current legislature, not the enacting one, that can overturn a decision, change the Court's jurisdiction, or alter the number of justices seated on the bench, the justices should be more concerned with how it may react to their decisions. These types of questions are also often posed during oral arguments.

An additional example is illustrative. In 1966, several members of Congress invoked the FOIA to compel disclosure of nine documents, prepared for the president, concerning a scheduled underground nuclear test. All but three of the documents were classified as Top Secret or Secret based on Executive Order 10501, and the EPA argued that the requested documents were interagency or intra-agency memoranda used in the executive branch's decision-making processes. Therefore the agency refused to produce the documents for the members of Congress. In *EPA v. Mink* (1973), the Court resolved this dispute and found in favor of the EPA. During the oral arguments, the justices inquired about whether Congress had set any FOIA exemptions that would allow members of Congress to obtain the files in question. The following exchange demonstrates that the justices were concerned with the exact nature of the regulations set out by Congress:

COURT: What significance would you give to the provisions of this legislation that provide for a *de novo* hearing in a district court and put the burden of proof on the government agency? Any at all?

COUNSEL: The significance is very considerable, under some of the exemptions of the act. I think the significance is much greater—

COURT: Well, with respect to this one, as you say, an *ex parte* affidavit and that's the end of it right?

COUNSEL: Congress has said that the matter is exempt and immune from disclosure

COURT: Well, it [Congress] has not said anything about—

COUNSEL: —if it's classified pursuant to an Executive Order, dealing with national defense information.

COURT: And here we have an *ex parte* affidavit am I right?

COUNSEL: That's right.

COURT: No opportunity for a court to determine whether or not, even if this was stamped secret or top secret?

COUNSEL: But absolutely no reason the affidavit itself, in its surrounding circumstances, to question the assertions of the affidavit itself. And the circumstances of the test, here we are dealing with a weapons test in the atomic field, in an area in which it is known that not only our technological lead, in the military field is vital to our national defense, but also in an area in which it's well known, because there are treaty obligations, because of the international—the sensitivity of the international community on these matters, where it is well known that there are foreign policy repercussions. And the Irwin affidavit places those documents plainly— the six to which exemption 1 applies—squarely within the core area of the interest that Congress intended to protect and remain privileged.

COURT: So, do I understand, then, that your answer to my question is that with respect to category 1, this language just be wholly disregarded, that the burden of proof is not on the government agency, and that the court has no business determining the matter *de novo* despite what Congress has enacted. (transcript of oral argument, 9–11)

Beyond gathering information about the power of Congress to set particular policies, the justices also raise questions about Congress's ability to constrain the Supreme Court's power by taking action such as limiting its jurisdiction to decide certain cases. *Marshall v. United States* (1974) focused on Title II of the Narcotic Addict Rehabilitation Act of 1966 (NARA), which prohibited inmates from entering a rehabilitation program if convicted of more than two felonies. Marshall argued that this law violated the equal protection of laws as outlined in the Fifth Amendment. During oral arguments, the justices inquired whether Congress really possessed the power to limit the discretion of federal courts to decide which inmates can be admitted to a rehabilitation program.

COURT: Does the power of Congress to fix the jurisdiction of federal courts constitute any kind of a barrier here to what you are driving at [that a district court can use discretion as to let a criminal get into a Title II rehab program]?

COUNSEL: Oh, I think certainly Congress could limit the jurisdiction of federal courts and provide that no addict could be committed for treatment. But where it has created a class, and a class to which Mr. Marshall is a member, and then excluded him from the class on the basis of an irrational classification, it is our position that he has been deprived of due process by virtue of the denial of equal protection . . .

COURT: Do I understand that you seem to concede the power of Congress to have a distinction between a distinction which permits the segregation of what you call hardened criminals, men with two, three, four, convictions, from first offenders who are narcotics addicts?

COUNSEL: Yes, Your Honor, I think they do. If they have a test that is fair and certainly a test that is not based upon a conclusive presumption of being a hardened criminal simply by virtue of two prior felony convictions . . . (transcript of oral argument, 17–19)

Ultimately, in *Marshall,* the Supreme Court ruled that Congress has the power to limit federal court jurisdiction. Combined with *Brown* and *Mink,* this demonstrates that the justices use oral arguments to determine how Congress might react to their decisions, as well as to ensure that they make decisions that respect congressional authority.

The justices also use oral arguments to raise questions about the executive branch's preferences and its possible reactions to decisions. A line of questions from the oral arguments in *United States v. Albertini* (1985) exemplifies this point. Because of past activities (mainly involving protests and the destruction of government property), Albertini was served with a bar letter prohibiting him from entering Hickman Air Force Base in Hawaii.[34] Ten years after the bar letter was sent, Albertini returned to the base during a ceremony open to the public and took pictures of a group peacefully demonstrating against the nuclear arms race. At that time the commanding officer identified Albertini and had him thrown off the base. Subsequently, Albertini was convicted for violating Title 18 U.S.C. 1382, which makes it unlawful to reenter a military base after having been "ordered not to reenter by any officer in command or charge thereof." The Court wanted to know when, if ever, a bar letter might expire and asked the assistant Solicitor General to explain the government's position:[35]

COUNSEL: I think the limitation on the duration of a bar letter is found not in section 1382, but in the requirement that administrative actions be reasonable. And therefore, a bar letter cannot extend beyond a reasonable time, and that is the limitation.

COURT: Do you have any idea what the government's position is on a reasonable time?

COUNSEL: I think it would necessarily depend on circumstances of each case. (transcript of oral argument, 7)

It is clear that the justices were concerned with the federal government's position on this issue, and it is easy to understand why they were interested. Indeed, if the Court regularly rules against the wishes of the present administration, the justices will be more likely to face sanctions from the executive branch (see chapter 1, as well as Epstein and Knight 1998a; Johnson 2003).

Congress and the executive branch are not the only actors who have interests at stake before the Court, and the justices are cognizant of this fact. As a result, the justices often ask questions about public opinion because it is important that the public view the Court as a legitimate institution.[36] Additionally, they probe the attorneys for information about state governments because states are often imbued with the authority to enforce a Court decision.

Wooley v. Maynard (1977) gave the justices the opportunity to consider public opinion on the First Amendment and to address the preferences of a state government. The issue in this case centered on a New Hampshire citizen's First Amendment right to tape over the state motto, "Live Free or Die," that was embossed on all motor vehicle license plates. Maynard and his wife, followers of the Jehovah's Witnesses faith, believed the motto violated their moral, religious, and political beliefs, and therefore chose to cover the motto. Maynard was found guilty in state court of violating the state law that made it a misdemeanor to block out the motto. Because he refused to pay the fine on three separate charges, he was sentenced to, and served, fifteen days in jail.

Justice Marshall used the oral arguments to raise questions about the public's stance on the motto issue, as well as about the state's position on the controversy.

MARSHALL: If everybody is in favor of getting rid of it [the state motto on license plates], you ought to get rid of it.

COUNSEL: This is not a burning issue within the state of New Hampshire. And this is one of the bases on which I would distinguish this case from the flag ones. Mr. Chief Justice Burger, in remarks this past summer, I believe, at a commencement address at one of our national universities . . .

COURT: Then, I understand the Attorney's General office does not have anything else to do that is why they brought it up here.

MARSHALL: Is it important in the state of NH or not?

COUNSEL: It is very important, Mr. Justice Marshall.

MARSHALL: But it is not a burning issue. (transcript of oral argument, 10)

I also argue that the Court can use oral arguments to determine the potential breadth of its decisions. That is, the justices can use this time to raise questions about the implications of a case in order to determine how the public and other governmental actors may view, and react to, their decisions. In *United States Postal Service v. Greenburgh Civic Associations* (1981) the Court was asked to determine whether Title 18 U.S.C. 1725, which prohibited the deposit of unstamped "mailable matter" in a letterbox approved by the United States Postal Service, violates a group's First Amendment right to disseminate information. During the oral arguments, Justice White inquired about the potential implications of deciding that the law was constitutional. He specifically wanted to know how far the law would reach if the Court upheld it.

WHITE: How about election circulars? Candidates? Has the statute been enforced against them?

COUNSEL: I believe that it has in a happenstantial fashion Mr. Justice White. In other words, there have been evidences—

WHITE: Well, your construction, in any event—if you win this case, there will be a good many other people besides civic associations that would benefit?

COUNSEL: I would believe that all noncommercial public interest and civic oriented material that would include certainly political candidates . . . (transcript of oral argument, 39)

Moreover, in *Seattle Times Co. v. Rhinehart* (1984) the Court delved into how a favorable decision for of the *Seattle Times* would affect the privacy interests, and the right to discovery, in future judicial proceedings.[37] One question in particular struck at the heart of determining the ramifications of the case:

Well, Mr. Edwards, if your position in your petition for *certiorari*, is correct that all these constitutional privacy interests are invaded by a discovery order, and Mr. Schwab's position that his clients' and all sorts of other clients' First Amendment interests are invaded if there is a protective order, then isn't Justice Stevens' earlier question to Schwab brought about in double, so to speak, that every single discovery order that a court makes is now a matter of federal constitutional import? (transcript of oral argument, 43)

Another way for the justices to determine the ramifications of choosing one decision over another is for them to pose hypothetical questions during oral arguments. These questions allow the justices to push counsel about how particular policy choices will hold up in slightly different circumstances and factual patterns. Biskupic (2000) argues that, even today, the justices are "masters of the hypothetical." Indeed, in *FDA v. Brown & Williamson Tobacco Corporation* (2000), the justices wanted to know how far the Food and Drug Administration's control may extend if the Court allowed it to regulate cigarettes. Justice Breyer viewed the issue as follows:

Suppose you get the thermal-glove-effect—warm hands—through a pill? Somebody says, "Take this pill it will toughen your skin and bring blood to your hands . . ." They say, "Take this pill, it's metabolized, it affects your brain, creates an addiction, and lo and behold, you've got warm hands if it gets cold in the winter . . ." Do you see what I mean? (quoted in Biskupic 2000, A17)

Similarly, Justice Scalia often asks questions that push the limits of a case, and Biskupic (2000, A17) notes that he "is known for his intricate legal scenarios that often come with a punch line." For instance, in a case involving the right to salvage a sunken ship, Scalia asked: "Suppose I drop a silver dollar down a grate, and I try to bring it up with a piece of gum on a stick and I can't do it, and I shrug my shoulders and walk off because I have not gotten it, and then somebody comes up and lifts up the grate and gets my silver dollar. Is that his silver dollar?" (quoted in Biskupic 2000, A17).

In my sample of cases, a question raised by Chief Justice Burger in *Zacchini v. Scripps Howard Broadcasting Co.* (1977) exemplifies his use of this tactic. This case came to the Supreme Court when a local television station broadcast his circus act (he was shot from a cannon), and Zacchini sued on the grounds that when people saw his act on television they would not pay to come and see it live. In legal terms, Zacchini argued that his act was his property, and therefore the television station could not broadcast it without permission or compensation. The Chief Justice wanted to know if this position would apply to all professional athletes whose performances were highlighted on television:

Let me pose a hypothetical to you, and I am going to ask your friend to comment on the same hypothetical later on when his turn comes. When Mohammed Ali engages in one of his professional exhibitions of prize fighting, I understand that the ratio is about ten to one or more that the TV rights are many many times the income he receives from the persons who are present at the arena. Suppose surreptitiously either one of the networks or an outlaw group filmed the entire fight and then tried to put it on the air. Do you analogize your client's situation to what that would be with Mohammed Ali? (transcript of oral argument, 16)

Together, these accounts provide empirical support for the data in table 2.4. They demonstrate that the justices ask many questions during oral arguments to gain information that may help them determine the preferences and possible reactions of relevant external actors. This is important because, to make efficacious and lasting policy choices, the justices must have some idea about how far they can push a decision, how others will react, whether their policy choices will stand up to the scrutiny of Congress, and how their choices may be implemented. The point is that other actors' preferences matter, the justices know this, and they utilize the oral arguments to gather such information because it is often not found in the litigant or *amicus* briefs.

THE COURT'S (LIMITED) FOCUS ON INSTITUTIONAL CONSTRAINTS. The justices focus much of their attention during oral arguments on those issue types that will help them decide cases as closely as possible to their preferred goals. However, they must also be wary of institutional constraints that may impede their ability to make certain decisions. In this section, I turn to my third information hypothesis—that justices should raise some questions about institutional constraints (defined as precedent and threshold issues), but fewer than they raise about policy and external actors' preferences. Turning back to table 2.4, it is evident that this is the case. The difference of means tests conducted above confirm that the Court is statistically less likely to ask these types of questions than to ask questions about policy or external actors' preferences. Given the expectations of the strategic model, however, the results are not as robust as I anticipated. Indeed, while the justices show some concern for precedent (9.8 percent of all questions asked in cases with *amici*, and 9.2 percent in cases without) and threshold issues (3.9 percent of all questions asked in cases with *amici* and 4.0 percent in cases without *amici*), the focus pales in comparison to the justices' questions about policy and external actors.

Existing literature provides insight about why the justices ask so few questions about precedent and threshold issues. For the former, Knight and Epstein (1996) show that the litigants' briefs often cite as many precedents as possible to the Court. Thus, it is possible that the justices do not have to raise many questions about precedent during the oral arguments. In other words, they may ask about *stare decisis* only when a controlling case is particularly important, or when the Court needs to clarify how that case relates to the one currently under consideration.[38] A similar explanation exists for the trivial number of threshold questions raised by the Court. The *certiorari* briefs almost always cover whether a case is ripe or moot, or whether a controversy actually exists. Further, Supreme Court Rule 24.1.e dictates that all briefs on the merits provide a jurisdictional statement. Thus, by the oral arguments, the justices may not need to concern themselves with either jurisdiction or issues of justiciability because the parties have already fleshed them out (in their *cert.* and merits briefs), and the Court has probably already discussed them (during *cert.* conference) before the oral arguments.[39]

In general, table 2.4 suggests that, during oral arguments, when the Court is able to elicit information without the filters attached to briefs, media coverage, or lower court decisions, justices focus on those issues that will help them act strategically. This means that the vast majority of their questions concern issues of policy, what other actors think about a case (including the public), how far a decision may reach, who will implement a decision, and how those who will implement a policy might interpret the decision. The key finding, then, is that Supreme Court justices use oral arguments to obtain information about policy and external actors, both of which help them make decisions that will end up close to their policy preferences.[40]

Individual-Level Behavior During Oral Arguments

While the Court as a whole seeks information that may be used for strategic purposes, can similar claims be made about individual justices? Initially, the logical answer may seem to be yes, considering the Court's overwhelming emphasis on policy and external actors' preferences during oral arguments. However, because individual-level inferences cannot be made based on aggregate data (see e.g., Huckfeldt and Sprague 1995; King 1997), it would be inappropriate to say that, during oral arguments, Justice Brennan seeks the same information as Justice Powell simply because the Court as a whole exhibits a particular behavior. Thus, in order to make claims about how individual justices utilize these proceedings, I must look to individual-level behavior. Unfortunately, few data exist to conduct such a test.

As argued in the data section, my solution to this problem is twofold. First, by using Justice Powell's bench notes, it is possible to determine what issues he thought were key to a case. This is not a perfect solution, because any analysis of Powell's behavior cannot be generalized to his brethren. However, an in-depth examination of the types of issues he found important during oral arguments may lend support to my aggregate findings. Indeed, if Powell acts in a manner consistent with the aggregate data, then there is even stronger support for the notion that oral arguments provide information to Supreme Court justices. For additional support, I use data from the *Landmark Briefs* series to determine how justices Stewart, White, and Brennan act during these proceedings. Together, these data allow me to go beyond the aggregate findings to explore how four individual justices utilize the oral arguments.

Initially, note Justice Powell's behavior during oral arguments. Table 2.5 demonstrates that his dominant concerns are the same as those of the Court as a whole; 42 percent of his notations focus on policy concerns, and 35 percent focus on external actors' preferences. In contrast, constitutional issues and questions about precedent or threshold issues garner little of Powell's attention.

The data from the analysis of Justices White, Stewart, and Brennan are equally compelling. While there is clearly variation in the types of questions

Table 2.5
Individual Justice's Behavior during Oral Arguments

Issue Type	Court[a]		Powell[b]		White[c]		Stewart[c]		Brennan[c]	
Constitutional	546	(10)	113	(14)	17	(13)	14	(14)	7	(11)
Policy	2,322	(42)	378	(47)	58	(44)	45	(47)	23	(37)
External Actors	1,946	(35)	148	(19)	46	(34)	18	(19)	25	(40)
Precedent	532	(9)	127	(16)	12	(9)	19	(20)	4	(7)
Threshold	221	(4)	29	(4)	0	(0)	0	(0)	3	(5)
Total	5,567	(100)	795	(100)	133	(100)	96	(100)	62	(100)

a = Aggregate Court data from 75 cases (questions asked in cases with *and* without *amici* participation).

b = Data are from Powell's notes taken during oral arguments in 75 cases (1972–86).

c = Data are from the oral arguments in 7 cases listed in *Landmark Briefs and Arguments* (Kurland and Casper 1975).

that they ask counsel, there is also evidence that they act in line with Powell and the Court as a whole. Indeed, policy concerns are the dominant focus of these three justices, as at least 37 percent of their questions focus on these issues. Additionally, with the exception of Justice Stewart, the second most prevalent concern for these justices is the preferences of actors beyond the Court. In general, Powell, White, Stewart, and Brennan exhibit behavior during oral arguments consistent with the aggregate findings in table 2.4. These individual-level data provide additional support for the first three hypotheses.

Expansion of the Written Record During Oral Arguments

So far I have shown that Supreme Court justices obtain specific types of information from oral arguments that may help them make decisions close to their preferred goals. This alone suggests that judicial scholars should reconsider whether these proceedings play a role in how the Court makes decisions. However, table 2.4 also provides a test for my final hypothesis, which is that oral arguments provide information to the justices beyond what they obtain from the litigant and *amicus* briefs.

I turn first to the general (non–issue specific) results. In cases with no *amicus* participation, only 20 percent of the Court's total questions focus on arguments initially discussed in the parties' briefs.[41] The remaining 80 percent of the

Court's questions raise issues that were not addressed in the litigants' written arguments. The presence of *amici* only decreases this number by three percentage points. In other words, even though the justices may have slightly more information going into the oral arguments (because *amici* are present), they are still more interested in obtaining additional information about a case than they are in clarifying the information provided to them by the litigants or *amici curiae*. A difference of means test between the number of new questions raised and the number of questions raised about briefed issues supports this conclusion. Indeed, the justices are significantly more likely to raise new issues than they are to ask about issues that are forwarded in a litigant or *amicus* brief (in both halves of the table, $p < .001$).

The overall number of new issues raised by the Court is staggering, and these findings hold for almost all of the individual issue types. With the exception of questions about constitutional issues, at least two-thirds of the Court's questions about each issue type raise concerns not addressed by the parties or *amici*.[42] Equally striking is that about 70 percent of all policy questions are raised for the first time during oral arguments. The difference between these questions and those that address policy issues first argued in the litigant or *amicus* briefs is also significant in both parts of table 2.4 ($p < .001$).

The other key findings from table 2.4 are the Court's emphasis on seeking new information about external actors and institutional rules. Almost 100 percent of its questions about the preferences or possible reactions of actors beyond the Court are raised for the first time during oral arguments. This is significantly greater than the number of questions that refer to briefed arguments about external actors' preferences ($p < .001$). The implication is that the briefs do not provide the justices with sufficient information about external actors. As such, the justices use the oral arguments to gather this vital information. Additionally, even when *amici* provide more information about external actors' preferences, the Court still seeks additional information.[43] This is also an important finding because, while the literature on *amicus curiae* participation indicates that these briefs provide the Court with an abundance of information about external actors' preferences (Epstein and Knight 1998b), the justices clearly use oral arguments to gather information beyond what even the *amici* provide.

Finally, in cases without *amici* almost 75 percent of questions about precedent are new, and this figure increases to over 80 percent when *amici* participate. Similarly, more than 68 percent of threshold issues are new when *amici* are not involved, while over 90 percent of the Court's questions about threshold issues are new when *amici* do file.[44] Considering that only about 13 percent of all arguments in the litigant and *amicus* briefs focus on these two issue types, this is clearly a significant emphasis during oral arguments. Again, the point is that the

Court has a norm respecting precedent (Knight and Epstein 1996) and rules governing when a case cannot be heard (Epstein and Knight 1998a). As such, the justices must ensure that they can make decisions close to their preferred goals while still following these institutional rules. Thus, although the justices focus few of their total questions on precedent and threshold issues, those they do raise focus on issues that were not fully briefed by the parties or *amici curiae*.

While what took place during oral arguments in *Roe* is only one example, it illustrates that the Court can and does use these proceedings to seek information beyond what is presented in the party's briefs. This is a common practice of the justices. As Justice Stevens put it:

> You often think of the oral arguments, you have a point in mind that you think may not have been brought out in the briefs well, that you want to be sure your colleagues don't overlook. You ask a question to bring it out. And you are not necessarily trying to sell everyone on the position but you want everyone to at least have the point in mind. (*America and the Courts* 1998)

Only one conclusion can be drawn from this analysis: oral arguments provide a plethora of information about policy issues, external actors' preferences, and institutional rules, as well as information that Supreme Court justices did not, or could not, obtain from the litigant or *amicus curiae* briefs. These findings support my fourth hypothesis, and cut deeply into the accepted view among judicial scholars that oral arguments play a limited role, at best, in the Court's decision-making process. The fact that justices seek new information during these proceedings indicates that oral arguments actually play a vital role for the Court. If the accepted view were correct, then the justices would not seek new information because they would not need any information beyond their personal preferences and the facts of the case (Segal and Spaeth 1993, 2002).

Conclusion

In the end, this chapter takes the first step toward demonstrating that oral arguments play a unique informational role in the Supreme Court's decision-making process. It suggests that the Court uses these proceedings to gain specific information about a given case. Two findings are notable. First, as policy-oriented and strategic actors, Supreme Court justices use their questions during oral arguments to determine the extent of their policy options, to help them form beliefs about the preferences of external actors, and to determine how these actors might react to their decisions. Second, the data suggest that the Court uses oral arguments to obtain information beyond that which is provided by the parties.

More generally, these findings should begin to change the way judicial scholars view the Court's entire decision-making process. Indeed, as Kassop (1993, 53) notes, scholars must strive to understand "how a case winds its intellectual way through the judicial process and on the contending positions that emerge at each juncture." The evidence presented here fills one of the key gaps in our understanding of this process by demonstrating that after briefs are submitted, and before the Court's conference discussions begin, the justices still seek information to help them make policy choices that accord with their preferences and to help them determine how other actors will react to their decisions.[45] The test of what they do with this information comes in chapters 4 and 5.

Chapter 3

⟐

Oral Arguments and
Coalition Formation

Introduction

On May 29, 1973, the Supreme Court announced its decision in *Columbia Broadcasting System v. Democratic National Committee*. The case originated when the Federal Communications Commission (FCC) issued an administrative decision against the Democratic National Committee (DNC). Specifically, the DNC brought a complaint to the FCC when a Columbia Broadcasting System (CBS) affiliate refused to sell the organization airtime meant for editorial advertisements intended to help raise money and promote the DNC's policy against the Vietnam War. The FCC ruled against the DNC and argued that a broadcaster who provides full and fair coverage of public issues does not have to sell airtime to "responsible entities" for editorial purposes.

Not to be deterred, the DNC appealed the administrative ruling to the Federal Court of Appeals for the D.C. Circuit. Although the circuit judges divided over the outcome, a majority agreed that the First Amendment forbids broadcasters from summarily refusing to sell time for people or groups to air editorial advertisements. As a result, the judges remanded the case in order for the FCC to develop procedures that would not violate the First Amendment. The Supreme Court granted *certiorari* to explicitly consider the First Amendment issue, and ultimately reversed the D.C. Circuit's decision. Writing for the majority, Chief Justice Burger argued that the basic criterion governing the use of broadcast frequencies is simply the right of the public to be informed. Thus, the Court ruled that if a broadcaster provides full and fair coverage, it is not bound to provide additional airtime for editorial advertisements.

While *CBS v. DNC* had important First Amendment implications, Justice Lewis F. Powell's behavior six months prior to the final outcome—during oral arguments—demonstrates another reason why these proceedings play an integral role in the Supreme Court's decision-making process. Indeed, an investigation of Justice Powell's oral argument notes in *CBS* (see chapter 2) indicates that he paid particular attention to the questions asked and comments made by Justices White and Stewart about whether this case actually implicated First Amendment jurisprudence. At one point during the arguments, Powell notes that "J. Stewart pointed out that . . . the respondent's argument is primarily an E/P [equal protection] argument rather than 1st Amendment" (Powell oral argument notes 1973, 8). Similarly he indicated Justice White's view on this issue: "J. White noted this is not an ordinary 1st Amendment case because we have here an *administrative agency* [emphasis in original]decision finding that free speech interests are best met by present regulatory system" (Powell oral argument notes 1973, 8).

Powell's personal—post-oral argument but preconference—notations suggest that he was intrigued about the issues raised by Stewart and White during these proceedings: "Argument suggests that the . . . issue may be E/P rather than Free Speech (see p8 these notes)."[1] Additionally, during conference discussion, Justice Douglas's notes, as well as Powell's own notes, demonstrate that Powell continued to think about the issue raised by Stewart and White. In fact, by the time conference concluded, Powell was leaning toward agreeing with their interpretation of the case: "I do not find state action issue as clear as other Justices. Yet, the arguments of Stewart and White are persuasive. I am impressed with view that in long run there will be greater free speech with a limited regulation of broadcast industry" (Powell conference notes in *CBS v. DNC*, October 20, 1972). Thus, it seems that Powell used the oral arguments to gather information about his colleagues' preferences and that he was ultimately persuaded by their arguments.[2]

Justice Powell's behavior suggests that, beyond allowing Supreme Court justices to gather information about external actors' preferences, oral arguments present the justices with an opportunity to learn about how their immediate colleagues want to decide specific cases. Providing evidence that justices use these proceedings for this purpose suggests that they do more than gather information from the litigants and *amici curiae*. Additionally, evidence that even one justice uses oral arguments to begin the coalition formation process when deciding a case (Maltzman, Spriggs, and Wahlbeck 2000) will go a long way toward showing that oral arguments play a specific and integral role in the strategic interaction that occurs between justices. Thus, in this chapter I systematically explore the extent to which Powell used oral arguments for this purpose in cases beyond *CBS v. DNC*.[3]

Decision Making under Risk, Cheap Talk, and Oral Arguments

In this section, I provide a theory of how oral arguments may help Supreme Court justices learn about their colleagues' preferences vis-à-vis specific cases. I begin with two assumptions beyond those outlined in chapter 1. First, most decisions by political actors are made under the condition of risk. Second, communication can decrease uncertainty about other actors' preferences. After delineating these assumptions, I apply them to Supreme Court decision making.

Decisions by political actors are made under a variety of information conditions. Sometimes actors have complete information about the state of the world (Gibbons 1992). Other decisions are made under risk, which means that an actor has incomplete information but can form beliefs about the probability that certain states of the world exist (Morrow 1994). More formally, Gibbons (1992, 143) argues that, "In a game of incomplete information . . . at least one player is uncertain about another player's payoff function." My first assumption, then, is that political actors often interact with one another under risk, which means they try to assess the probability that other actors hold certain preferences.

Second, I assume that political actors need information to help them make probability assessments about other actors' preferences (Gibbons 1992; Morrow 1994). While this information can come from many sources, game theoretic literature indicates that under certain conditions cheap talk—defined as costless signals sent between political actors—is an effective method of communication (Morrow 1994; Farrell 1987; Crawford and Sobel 1982). To understand why cheap talk signals can help actors coordinate with one another for their mutual benefit, initially consider when these signals may be uninformative: if all the actors in a game believe that their signals will be ignored, then nobody will listen to or believe the information contained in the signals (Farrell 1987). Ultimately, cheap talk signals will not help actors coordinate in this scenario, and therefore they will have no effect on the outcome of the interaction. As a result, Farrell (1987, 35) points out that "it is optimal (among other things) for each player to make his claims uncorrelated from his actions."

Although cheap talk provides uninformative information under the above conditions, there are times when it can help actors coordinate strategies for their mutual benefit (Farrell 1987; Farrell and Gibbons 1986; Farrell and Saloner 1985; Crawford and Sobel 1982). Farrell (1987) suggests that if all players expect to reach a state of equilibrium, and if they will follow the equilibrium once it is announced, then "cheap talk can help coordinate behavior to produce . . . equilibria" (35). In short, actors can coordinate so that each attains his or her most preferred outcomes. This condition, however, is necessary but not sufficient for cheap talk to be effective. Indeed, Crawford and Sobel (1982) indicate that players' preferences must also coincide with one another for coordination to occur (Crawford and Sobel 1982). As Lupia and McCubbins (1998) explain, "[P]ersuasion does not occur if the principal believes that the speaker is likely to have conflicting interests. If, however, the principal believes that common interests are more likely, then persuasion is possible" (50).

I assume that cheap talk helps actors coordinate on two levels. First, based on the above literature, I argue that it allows coordination between actors with similar preferences because it is inherently easier for them to agree than it is for actors with divergent views to do so. For example, Morrow (1994) notes that legislative debate "provides a way for legislators with similar underlying preferences to coordinate their votes," because "[m]embers are unlikely to take cues from those whose underlying values are greatly different from their own" (256). More generally, scholars demonstrate that, theoretically and empirically, this is a necessary condition in order for actors to coordinate with another through cheap talk signals (Lupia and McCubbins 1998; Crawford and Sobel 1982).

Second, I extend cheap talk theory by arguing that it can help actors coordinate when groups make decisions under majority rule—where the median almost always must join a coalition in order for it to be a winning coalition (Black 1958; Martin 2001). Although extant cheap talk literature does not specifically address communication in this manner, I argue that these signals provide one mechanism by which actors can learn the preferences of the pivotal voter because all actors in a group likely share some common interests with the median. As such, they can use the median's cheap talk signals to assess her preferences, and then use these messages when trying to build a majority coalition. The general point, however, applies to both of my assumptions: for cheap talk to help actors coordinate, it is necessary that they at least perceive that they share common interests.

Recent research suggests that the game theoretic assumption about decisions made under risk applies to the Supreme Court. Indeed, there are several reasons to believe that Supreme Court justices do not always know how their colleagues want to act in specific cases. First, justices' preferences can and do change over time (Epstein et al. 1998). Second, justices' preferences vary across issue areas (Epstein et al. 1996). Third, most cases tap multiple issue dimensions (Spaeth 2003), which creates ambiguity about which dimension is controlling (Maltzman and Wahlbeck 1996a). This combination of factors suggests that even though justices may be able to generally predict their colleagues' preferences, they may often possess some uncertainty about how their colleagues want to act in particular cases (Maltzman, Spriggs, and Wahlbeck 2000).

Due to this uncertainty, justices must procure information about their colleagues' views concerning specific cases if they are to reach decisions that end up as close as possible to their preferred outcomes. While existing literature indicates that many opportunities exist for justices to gather this information (*cert*. votes in the present case [Caldeira, Wright, and Zorn 1999], past merits votes in similar cases [Maltzman, Spriggs, and Wahlbeck 2000]), oral arguments provide an important forum for them to do so.[4] To see why, I consider oral arguments as a forum for cheap talk between the justices where each question and comment from a justice signals his preferences to the rest of the Court.[5] More specifically, justices often use these proceedings to help coordinate with one another about the final policy outcomes of cases that they hear.

This is consistent with the way judicial scholars and appellate-level attorneys view oral arguments. For instance, Wasby, D'Amato, and Metrailer (1977) argue that "it is not surprising that the judges would use part of the oral argument time for getting across obliquely to their colleagues on the bench arguments regarding the eventual disposition of a case" (xviii). They conclude elsewhere that "Another, less noticed function is that oral argument serves as a means of communication between judges" (Wasby, D'Amato, and Metrailer 1976, 418). Additionally, Cooper (1995) points out that conflict between the justices over how to decide a given case begins during oral arguments.

Appellate-level advocates agree with these scholarly accounts. Shapiro (1984, 547) posits, "During the heat of debate on an important issue, counsel may find that one or more justices are especially persistent in questioning and appear unwilling to relent. This may be the case when a justice is making known his or her views in an emphatic manner." Neuborne goes a step further and suggests that he often feels like an intermediary between the justices when he appears at oral argument: "Sometimes I think I am a post office. I think that one of the justices wants to send a message to another justice and they are essentially arguing through me" (*This Honorable Court* 1988).[6]

The justices themselves confirm the assessments of scholars and attorneys. Justice Breyer points out that "[during oral arguments] the Court is having a conversation with itself through the intermediary of the attorney" (*America and the Courts* 1998). Justice Scalia agrees: "It isn't just an interchange between counsel and each of the individual justices; what is going on is to some extent an exchange of information among justices themselves" (*This Honorable Court* 1988). In short, justices, attorneys, and scholars who study oral arguments agree that questions during these proceedings act as signals to the rest of the Court about the preferences of the questioner.

Drawing on the assumptions about decisions under risk and cheap talk, along with their application to the Supreme Court, I test two hypotheses about how justices use oral arguments in the coalition formation process. First, as noted above, for cheap talk to be effective it is necessary for actors to have some common interests (Crawford and Sobel 1982; Farrell 1987). This leads me to the following hypothesis:

> **Cheap Talk Hypothesis 1: Justices use oral arguments to assess messages sent by those who are closer to them ideologically more often than to assess the messages of those who are ideologically distant from them.**[7]

Second, the median justice is almost always needed for a majority coalition to form (Murphy 1964), and almost always shares some common interests with each member of the Court. Thus, I also hypothesize the following:

> **Cheap Talk Hypothesis 2: Justices use oral arguments to assess the median justice's policy preferences significantly more often than those of other justices.**

Data and Methods

To test the above hypotheses, I constructed a unique data set that relies on notes taken by Justice Lewis F. Powell during oral arguments in a random sample of cases decided between 1972 and 1986.[8] These notes are significant because they provide an explicit measure of learning for Justice Powell (for an example of these notes see appendix 3). In other words, I argue that he wrote down a colleague's question or comment only when he believed that he could learn something about her preferences. In turn, I posit that he used this knowledge to determine which justices were most likely to help him form a viable majority coalition. More generally, these notes provide a unique opportunity to study how political actors learn about other actors' preferred outcomes. Given that scholars have rarely studied how political actors do so, Powell's notes offer significant insight into the key behind strategic interaction.[9]

I coded every unique paragraph in Powell's notes to determine the type of information included in them, and whether Powell attributed what was said to one of his colleagues. This resulted in a sample of 1,567 unique paragraphs, of which 193 explicitly referenced policy questions, statements, or positions taken by Powell's colleagues during the oral arguments.[10] Although the coding scheme is highly subjective, the results are quite reliable.[11]

The data set includes an observation for each justice in every case in the sample. The dependent variable, then, is a count of the total number of notations made by Justice Powell about each justice's statements per case. Because this is a discrete measure, I cannot use traditional linear regression to model this phenomenon. As Long (1994, 217) points out, "The use of LR models for count outcomes can result in inefficient, inconsistent, and biased estimates." A reasonable alternative is the negative binomial regression model (Greene 1997, 931).[12]

The model contains several independent variables. Table 3.1 provides summary statistics for them, as well as for the dependent measure. To test the first hypothesis, I use Epstein et al.'s (1996) twelve-category scheme to calculate the absolute difference between Powell's issue-specific ideology and the ideology of each of his colleagues.[13] In other words, for each issue area I subtract the percentage of cases that Powell voted liberally from the percentage of cases that each colleague voted liberally. I also include a variable to test the hypothesis that

Table 3.1
Variables Affecting Justice Powell's Decision to Note his Colleagues' Questions and Comments during Oral Arguments

Variable	Mean	Min	Max	SD	Valid Observations	Hypothesized Direction
Does Powell note colleague's question?	0.20	0.00	7.00	0.57	979	
Ideological proximity to Powell	19.59	2.50	45.30	15.42	979	−
Distant of each justice from the median	2.29	0.00	4.00	1.40	979	−
Powell and colleague have a new relationship	0.17	0.00	1.00	0.38	979	+
Physical proximity between Powell and colleague during oral arguments	3.91	1.00	8.00	2.25	979	−
Mean number of questions asked during oral arguments	13.56	4.77	21.02	5.78	854	+

Data Sources: Powell Archives, Washington and Lee School of Law, Lexington, Va.; Epstein et al. (1996); Schubert et. al (1991a); portraits of the Supreme Court.

Powell should be more concerned with questions raised by the median justice than with questions raised by his more ideologically extreme colleagues. Specifically, using the ideological distance variable I determine the proximity of each justice to the median; the median justice is coded 0, the two justices closest to him are coded 1, and so on for each justice on the Court.[14] Because I am interested in the ideological proximity between Powell and his colleagues, I expect both of these variables to have a negative and significant relationship with his decision to note a colleague's question or comment from the oral arguments.

I also include three variables to control for possible alternative explanations for Powell's behavior. First, to test whether he is more interested in learning about the preferences of colleagues with whom he has worked for only a few years, I create a dummy variable that equals 1 for the first two years that Powell is on the bench with a particular justice, and 0 for the rest of their combined tenure on the Court.[15] In Powell's first two full terms (1972 and 1973), cases assume a value of 1 for each justice, while cases beginning in the 1974 term are all coded 0. For justices who join the Court later than Powell (O'Connor and Stevens), this variable is coded 1 for cases in the new justice's first two terms (1981 and 1982 for O'Connor), and 0 for all cases thereafter.

Second, I assess whether Powell is more inclined to cite comments made by those justices who are the most prolific questioners during oral arguments. To do so I employ a proxy variable drawn from Schubert et al. (1992), which measures the mean number of questions each justice asks for a random sample of cases in each term.[16] Although not an ideal measure, these are the only existing data that give insight into how many questions each justice asks, on average, during oral arguments.

Finally, I include a variable to capture whether Powell is more inclined to note questions asked by justices who sit nearest to him during oral arguments. To determine the seating order on the bench, I utilize the portraits of the Court for each natural Court in the sample.[17] The argument for including this as a control variable is that Powell may have an easier time hearing questions raised by those who sit closer to him during the arguments. More generally, while the Court uses microphones during these proceedings, it may be easier for justices to hear questions asked by those who sit directly next to them than by those who sit farther away.[18]

Results

Table 3.2 provides the results of the analysis.[19] In line with the first hypothesis, Powell is significantly more likely to note comments made by colleagues who are closer to his own preferences (p = .01). This comports with the cheap talk

Table 3.2
Negative Binomial Regression Estimates of Justice Powell's Decision to Note his Colleagues' Questions and Comments during Oral Arguments

Variables	Coefficient	Robust Standard Error	Significance
Constant	−1.31	0.75	0.08
Ideological proximity of justice to Powell	−0.02	0.01	0.01
Distance of justice from the median	−0.18	0.10	0.07
Powell and colleague have a new relationship	0.04	0.28	0.87
Physical proximity between Powell and colleague during oral arguments	−0.13	0.09	0.15
Mean number of questions asked during oral arguments	0.05	0.02	0.03
α (alpha)[a]	2.32	0.78	0.01
N	854		
Log likelihood	−379.93		
Wald χ^2 (5 d.f.)	41.10		0.00

a The alpha coefficient provides a test of whether the negative binomial or the Poisson is the appropriate modeling choice (see note 19 for an explanation).

literature that suggests it is easier to send and receive messages, which may help two actors coordinate, when their preferences are similar. More generally, it is clear that Powell was more concerned with the oral argument questions raised by colleagues with ideologically similar views, as over 20 percent of all his notes refer to members of the conservative faction on the Court (defined as Burger, Rehnquist, and O'Connor).

Powell's interest in Chief Justice Burger's comments during the arguments in *Kelley v. Johnson* (1976) illustrates these findings. In 1971 Johnson brought a civil rights action (under 42 U.S.C. 1983) against the commissioner of the Suffolk County Police Department. The suit came to light after the commissioner established hair-grooming standards (applicable only to men) focused on the style and length of hair, sideburns, and mustaches. Further, the regulations banned beards and goatees, except in the case of medical necessity. Johnson and the Suffolk County Patrolmen's Benevolent Association attacked the regulation as violating the right to free expression under the First Amendment and the guarantees of due process and equal protection under the Fourteenth Amendment. The specific argument was that the regulations were "not based upon the generally accepted standard of grooming in the community" and that they placed "an undue restriction" upon police officers' personal activities (majority opinion, 240).

During the oral arguments in *Johnson*, Justice Powell was particularly interested in a point raised by Chief Justice Burger. He wrote, "The CJ noted that police are not allowed to make political speech and said this limitation on speech is more direct than the limitation here" (Powell oral argument notes, 2). In short, according to Powell, Burger did not seem to think the regulation was an undue burden on police officers' First Amendment rights. For my purposes, it demonstrates that Powell was concerned with the preferences of one of his ideologically compatible colleagues—which comports with the cheap talk thesis and my hypothesis about how justices utilize oral arguments to begin building viable majority coalitions.

Additionally, and as predicted, Powell is significantly more likely to note questions and comments raised by colleagues ideologically close to the median justice than he is to note comments of justices farther away from the median ($p = 0.07$). Powell's behavior in *CBS v. DNC* illustrates his clear interest in the questions and comments made by the two justices who were the medians for the majority of the cases in my sample. The raw data confirm that his interest in their comments was not relegated to *CBS* only. Indeed, over 50 percent ($N = 97$) of all Powell's oral argument notes about his colleagues' preferences refer to points made by Justices White and Stewart. If I include the other members of the Burger Court's "moderate" wing (Blackmun and Stevens), this percentage increases to over 70 percent ($N = 136$). The implication is that Powell knew he needed the median's vote to secure a majority and therefore paid more attention to the questions and comments of this pivotal justice.

Only one of the three alternative explanations has a significant effect on Powell's choice of whose questions and comments to note—how prolific a justice is at asking questions during oral arguments. Neither the physical proximity of a justice, nor the fact that Powell and a colleague have only been on the Court together for a short time, has an effect on Powell's behavior. So while there is evidence that Powell's choices include nonstrategic elements, the model indicates that this calculation includes a clear strategic component. That is, he is more likely to note oral argument questions or comments of colleagues who can help him form a majority coalition.

Because it is difficult to interpret the substantive meaning of the coefficients in table 3.2, I also generated predicted probabilities for Powell's behavior. When all of the variables are held constant at their mean or modal values, the probability of Powell noting any single colleague's comments is 14 percent. With this baseline, I consider the probabilities based on a justice's ideological proximity to Powell. Here the probability of Powell making at least one notation for the justice closest to himself ideologically is 20 percent, while the probability for the farthest justice is 9 percent. Second, I compare the predicted probabilities for different distances from the median. It is clear that the closer a justice is to the median, the more likely Powell will note her question or comment. Indeed, the probability jumps to 20 percent for comments made by the median justice, and drops to 11 percent for the two justices farthest from the median. Finally, note that the probability jumps to 26 percent if the justice making the comment is the median justice and is closest ideologically to Powell, and it increases to 42 percent if that justice also asks the most questions during the oral arguments. The interpretation of these variables suggests that, substantively, Powell's choice of whose comments to note is at least partially strategic.

Information and Coalition Formation

The results from the previous section suggest that at least one justice on the Supreme Court utilized oral arguments to learn how his colleagues wanted to act in certain cases. However, if Justice Powell gathered this information but did not use it when trying to build majority coalitions, then I could not argue that he strategically gathered this information. As such, I turn to the additional question of whether this information ultimately helped Powell build coalitions. Specifically, I hypothesize that there should be a significant relationship between the number of times per case that Powell notes a colleague's oral argument comments and the propensity for Powell and that colleague to join the same coalition.[20]

To test this hypothesis, I compare the data from Powell's oral argument notes with data from the final votes on the merits for each case in the sample. If such a relationship exists, then there is evidence that, at least for one justice, oral arguments play an informational role in the coalition formation process that takes place on the Supreme Court. The dependent variable is coded 1 if Powell and a colleague join the same coalition, and 0 otherwise.[21] The key independent variable is the number of times Powell notes comments made by

Table 3.3
Logit Estimates of the Propensity for
Justice Powell and Colleague to Join the Same Coalition

Variables	Coefficient	Standard Error	Significance (One-Tailed Test)
Constant	−0.76	0.22	0.00
Number of cites to colleague's oral argument comments	0.21	0.16	0.10
Colleague and Powell in same conference coalition	3.12	0.19	0.00
Colleague's ideological distance from Powell	−0.04	0.01	0.00
Colleague's distance from the median	0.12	0.08	0.07
N	907		
Model χ^2	406.50		0.00

each colleague during oral arguments (the dependent variable in the first model). Table 3.3 presents the results from the logistic regression analysis.

Even when controlling for three highly plausible alternative explanations, a significant relationship persists between the number of times Powell cites a colleague's oral argument comments and the propensity for him to join the same final coalition ($p = 0.10$). Substantively, while there is an 86 percent probability that Powell and a given colleague will join the same coalition when all the variables are held at their mean or modal values, this probability reaches 95 percent if Powell makes five citations to a colleague's oral argument comments. Further, if he cites seven comments from oral arguments, then there is a 97 percent chance that he and that colleague will join the same coalition.[22] This demonstrates that a justice is substantively more likely to join the same coalition as Powell when Powell pays more attention to that colleague's policy questions and comments during oral arguments.

These findings indicate that, at least indirectly, oral arguments play an independent role in the coalition formation process on the Supreme Court. While I cannot make specific claims about how Powell used this information, the evidence suggests that he learned about his colleagues' preferences and then used what he learned to facilitate coordination with his colleagues during the Court's opinion-writing stage. In other words, the oral arguments helped Powell decrease his uncertainty about his colleagues' preferences, which ultimately helped him determine how to build coalitions when making decisions.

Conclusions and Implications

Generally, this chapter takes an important step toward helping scholars understand the process through which Supreme Court justices learn about their colleagues' preferences and how they use what they learn to build viable majority coalitions with one another. Clearly, justices have many opportunities to gather this information—votes on *certiorari* (Boucher and Segal 1995), past votes (Epstein et al. 1996), and conference discussions (Epstein and Knight 1998a). However, there are times when justices may need additional information about how their colleagues want to act in specific cases. The evidence here demonstrates that, at least for one justice, the oral arguments provide an additional mechanism through which such information may flow. That is, these proceedings present another opportunity for the justices to learn about their colleagues' preferences. This also adds a key piece of the puzzle about why oral arguments are vitally important for the Supreme Court and why the justices take them so seriously.

While my findings cannot say definitively that all justices use oral arguments as a means to learn about their colleagues' preferred outcomes, they suggest that these proceedings provide at least one justice with information that helps him do so. To make more definitive claims, additional research is required to determine whether these findings hold for other issue areas, other Court eras, and other justices. However, there is no theoretical reason to suspect that other justices would act differently, because every justice must learn about her colleagues' preferences in order to obtain the votes necessary to make good law. Additionally, given that Court scholars know next to nothing about how justices use oral arguments, these data go a long way toward providing an explanation of how these proceedings allow justices to learn about their colleagues' preferences over how to decide specific cases. Finally, given what we know about the strategic nature of justices' behavior at other stages of the decision-making process (*certiorari* decisions, opinion assignment, opinion writing), it is reasonable to assume that they also act in this manner during oral arguments.

In the end, the findings here support the theoretical claim about why oral arguments are particularly important for the Court: they provide necessary information that helps justices learn about how their colleagues want to act so that they can more effectively build coalitions when deciding on the merits of a case. This is important for judicial scholars as well as for those who study other institutions such as Congress, the executive branch, and the bureaucracy. Indeed, the findings suggest that political actors can inform themselves through verbal communication—sometimes in the form of cheap talk—and then use this information so that they can try to place policy outcomes as close as possible to their own preferred goals.

Chapter 4

———⇒•⇐———

Conference, Opinion Writing, and Oral Arguments

Introduction

E pstein and Kobylka (1992) point out that after the initial oral arguments in *Roe v. Wade,* "The justices returned to their chambers with little more than when they had left" (182). Given that "none of the original majority had changed their votes" after the rehearing (Epstein and Kobylka 1992, 192), this analysis suggests that the oral arguments in *Roe* played little role in how the Court decided the case. There is evidence, however, that during the Court's conference discussion and opinion-writing process, the justices were concerned with the legal and policy implications of when a state's interest in protecting life outweighs a woman's right to obtain an abortion on demand (see the introduction in chapter 2). Indeed, in his conference notes, Justice Brennan indicates that Justices Stewart and Marshall specifically raised this issue after the second round of arguments. According to Brennan, Stewart argued that a "State can legislate to extent of requiring doctors, that after certain point of pregnancy, can't have abortion etc." Brennan also notes Marshall's concerns: "Go with WOD but time problem concerns me—why can state prevent in early stages but why can't state prohibit after certain stage" (Brennan conference notes, *Roe v. Wade,* October 13, 1972).

After the second conference in *Roe* it was also evident that the timing issue continued to be a point of discussion for Justice Blackmun (the majority opinion writer) as well as for the entire Court. In a memorandum to conference Blackmun told his colleagues, "You will observe that I have concluded that the end of the first trimester is critical. This is arbitrary, but perhaps any other selected point, such as quickening or viability, is equally arbitrary" (November 21, 1972). In a subsequent memorandum, dated December 4, 1972, Blackmun

71

outlined exactly why he supported using the first trimester as the cutoff instead of some other point in the pregnancy:

> I could go along with viability if it could command a court. By that time the state's interest has grown large indeed. I suspect that my preference, however, is to stay with the end of the first trimester for the following reasons: (1) It is more likely to command a court; (2) A state is still free to make its decision on the liberal side and fix a later point in the abortion statutes it enacts; (3) I may be wrong, but I have the impression that many physicians are concerned about facilities and, for example, the need for hospitalization after the first trimester. I would like to leave the states free to draw their own medical conclusions with respect to the period after three months and until viability. The states' judgment of the health needs of the mother, I feel, ought, on balance, to be honored. (memo to conference, December 4, 1972)

Blackmun's analysis sparked a number of responses concerning the balance of interests—several which are notable. As during conference, Marshall was clearly troubled by this issue, and initially argued that he was unwilling to support a policy based on the trimester scheme. In a memorandum dated December 12, he wrote to Blackmun (and the conference):

> I am inclined to agree that drawing the line at viability accommodates the interests at stake better than drawing it at the end of the first trimester. . . . It is implicit in your opinion that at some point the State's interest in preserving the potential life of the unborn child overrides any individual interests of the women. I would be disturbed if that point were set before viability, and I am afraid that the opinion's present focus on the end of the first trimester would lead states to prohibit abortions completely at any later date. (memo to conference, December 12, 1972)

A day after Marshall circulated his memorandum, Justice Powell weighed in on the first trimester versus viability debate. He wrote, "Once we take the major step of affirming a woman's constitutional right, it seems to me that viability is a more logical and defensible time for identifying the point at which the state's overriding right to protect potential life becomes evident." Powell goes on to state that he would rely on the second Circuit's opinion to help bolster his point: "I was favorably impressed by the CA 2 opinion (Judges Newman and Lumbard) in *Abele* which identified viability as the critical time from the viewpoint of the state" (memo to conference, December 13, 1972).

These memoranda indicate clear disagreement among the justices about how to distinguish when a woman's interest in obtaining an abortion ends and the state's interest in protecting the life of a fetus begins. More important for my thesis, however, is that this issue stemmed directly from a question raised by the Court during oral arguments. As such, this anecdote demonstrates that the justices can and do discuss issues raised during oral arguments in their conference discussions and in memoranda sent between chambers during the opinion-writing process.

This chapter explores whether Supreme Court justices generally discuss information that they obtain from the oral arguments during conference proceedings and the opinion-writing process, or whether *Roe* is an anomaly. To do so, I compare the conference notes and intra-Court memoranda with the oral argument transcripts and legal briefs. This comparison allows me to determine the extent to which the justices actually discuss issues from the oral arguments during their decision-making process. If, during their internal deliberations, the justices' comments focus on information from the oral arguments, then evidence exists to support the claim that these proceedings play an informational role in the Court's decision-making process. The crux of the analysis focuses on conference discussions; I then briefly analyze the discussion of such information during the opinion-writing process.

Hypotheses

In their article "The Norm of Stare Decisis," Knight and Epstein (1996) argue, "One important source of evidence in support of the existence of a norm of *stare decisis*, we believe, is the extent to which justices invoke precedent in their arguments during the private conferences . . . The very fact that precedent would be employed as a source of persuasion in their *private* communications suggests that the justices believe that it can have an effect on the choices of their colleagues" (1024). Knight and Epstein conclude that, because the justices discuss precedent in their internal deliberations, *stare decisis* plays a key role in the Court's decision-making process. Although they claim that their data are a "modest and indirect" (1032) means of supporting their theory, they argue that these findings corroborate their claims. I agree. That the justices discuss certain issues during their private deliberation process suggests that, outside of public scrutiny, they believe these issues warrant serious attention as they try to arrive at substantive legal and policy decisions.

The logic behind Knight and Epstein's findings is applicable to my analysis of oral arguments. Justices' public statements (see chapter 1) indicate that these proceedings provide invaluable information that helps them make decisions, but it is difficult to determine the extent to which these statements actually translate into the efficacy of oral arguments in the Court's decision-making process. Indeed, justices may use these public statements to justify the time they spend discussing a case in open court, to demonstrate that anyone can have their case heard by the highest court in the land, or to show that the Court is not as secretive as it is sometimes portrayed to be. In short, it is difficult to determine the accuracy of such statements.

Analyzing the nonpublic portions of the Court's decision-making process gives me the leverage to do so. In line with Knight and Epstein's (1996) analysis of *stare decisis,* I argue that if the justices actually scrutinize information from the oral arguments during their private discussions—that is, during conference—then there is merit to what they say publicly about the importance and usefulness of oral arguments as an information gathering tool. This leads to my first hypothesis:

> **Conference Hypothesis 1: If oral arguments play an informational role in how the Court makes substantive legal and policy decisions, then a significant proportion of the issues justices discuss during conference should emanate from oral arguments.**

If the justices only discuss issues from oral arguments that clarify briefed arguments, then, although I can claim that these proceedings play a role in how the Court decides cases, I cannot argue that they play a unique informational role in this process. I must also provide evidence that the justices discuss issues raised during oral arguments that are not addressed in writing by the litigant or *amicus curiae* briefs—as was the case in *Roe.* Chapter 2 demonstrates that the vast majority of information the justices elicit from counsel during oral arguments is not part of the major arguments found in either the litigant or *amicus* briefs. In line with Knight and Epstein's arguments, if this information helps the Court make decisions, then the justices should discuss it during conference. Thus, I also hypothesize the following:

> **Conference Hypothesis 2: If the oral arguments play a *unique* informational role for the Court, then a significant proportion of all references to these proceedings during conference should focus on issues that are raised by the justices during the oral arguments but that the litigants and *amici curiae* did not address in their briefs.**

So far I have made general predictions about how I expect the Court to deal with issues from the oral arguments during conference. In addition, and in line with the strategic theory of decision making explicated in chapter 1, I also expect the justices to focus on information that will help them reach decisions as close as possible to their preferred outcomes. Specifically, during oral arguments the justices clearly pay attention to policy issues, the preferences of external actors, and, to a lesser extent, institutional rules. These findings lead me to conclude that Supreme Court justices use oral arguments to gather information that will help them act strategically. If oral arguments, in turn, play a unique role in helping the justices accomplish this goal, I hypothesize the following:

Conference Hypothesis 3: When discussing policy issues, focusing on external actors' preferences, and invoking institutional rules during conference, the majority of these arguments should be discussed during the oral arguments, and a significant proportion should originate uniquely during these proceedings.

Finally, I am interested in the Court's use of information from the oral arguments during the opinion-writing process. Maltzman, Spriggs, and Wahlbeck (2000) demonstrate that, after conference, justices act strategically when trying to reach agreeable substantive outcomes in a case. That is, justices realize their decisions depend on how each of their colleagues wants to decide a case. I analyze this aspect of the Court's decision-making process to gain additional leverage on the extent to which the justices utilize information from oral arguments, as they make legal and policy choices. The post-conference bargaining in *Roe* indicates that the justices do, at times, discuss issues from the oral arguments in their intra-Court memoranda. Thus, just as they do during conference, I expect justices to discuss issues in these memoranda that were raised during oral arguments and that will help them decide cases as closely as possible to their preferred goals. Thus, my fourth hypothesis is as follows:

Opinion-Writing Hypothesis: If oral arguments provide information that helps the justices reach their preferred outcomes, then they should discuss issues from these proceedings in their memoranda sent during the opinion-writing process.

Data and Methods

To test the above hypotheses, I compare issues from the briefs and the oral argument transcripts with the conference notes and memoranda found in the case files of Justices Powell, Brennan, and Douglas. I employ the same coding scheme from chapter 2 to discern which issues are discussed during conference, how often they are discussed, and from where they originate (see pages 32–35).

Because I have records of each justice's conference comments, as well as all memos sent in each case, I analyze both aggregate Court behavior and whether the propensity to discuss issues from oral arguments varies among justices.

To obtain the most accurate picture of what transpired during conference, I utilize all three sets of conference notes and code every unique remark that was recorded. However, I do not double code the remarks. Thus, if Justices Brennan and Douglas both indicate that Justice Powell raised a particular point, I code it only once. I also follow a convention utilized by Epstein and Knight (1998a) in that I do not use any of the justices' own written statements to determine their personal conference remarks.[1] For instance, I rely on the notes taken by Douglas and Powell to determine comments made by Brennan. I do so to ensure a degree of comparability across the Court.

To code conference memoranda, I employ a similar procedure. Using Court papers from Justice Powell's and Justice Brennan's files, I copied all memos sent either privately or to the entire conference for every case in my sample. I then compared these memoranda with the briefs and oral argument transcripts to determine the types of issues and their origin. Note that I do not include any memoranda that simply say "Please join me in your decision," or circulated opinion drafts. Rather, I code only memoranda that included substantial discussion of the issues in a case.

A comparison of the briefs, oral arguments transcripts, and the justices' internal deliberations provides a good means to test the informational role oral arguments play in the Court's decision-making process. If the Court as a whole, and a majority of individual justices, invoke issues from oral arguments, and specifically information from these proceedings that will help them attain their most preferred policy goals, then there is evidence oral arguments play an informational role in the Court's decision-making process.[2]

Results

This section explores the extent to which the Supreme Court discusses information from oral arguments during conference and the opinion-writing process. First, I conduct an analysis of aggregate Court behavior to determine whether conference discussion revolves around briefed issues that the justices sought to clarify during oral arguments, or whether it revolves around issues the justices added to the record during these proceedings. Second, I determine whether variation exists in the extent to which individual justices raise issues from oral arguments during conference discussions. Third, I analyze the extent to which oral arguments provide the justices with information about their policy options, external actors' preferences, and institutional rules. Finally, I turn to memoranda sent between the justices after conference to determine how often information from oral arguments is invoked in bargaining statements sent between chambers.

The Court's Discussion of Information from Oral Arguments during Conference

To test the first hypothesis, I initially compare the questions asked by the Court during these proceedings with the conference notes of Justices Brennan, Powell, and Douglas. Such a comparison allows me to assess the Court's overall focus on issues the justices actually discuss during the oral arguments. At first blush, there is clear variation from case to case as to how much the justices focus on oral arguments. The discussion of orally argued issues ranges from no comments—in two cases—to a peak of twenty-six comments made in *First National Bank of Boston v. Bellotti* (1978).[3] Additionally, the justices discuss an average of eleven issues from oral arguments per case (SD = 5.92). That the justices discuss more than five orally argued issues, even one standard deviation below the mean, suggests the justices have obtained information from these proceedings that they think is important for making substantive decisions in a case. Table 4.1 presents more explicit data about the origin of issues justices discuss during conference.

In both halves of this table, the justices rarely discuss issues raised in the legal briefs that they do not ask about during oral arguments. Specifically, only 5 percent of the issues discussed during conference are found exclusively in the briefs when *amici* do not participate, while less than 1 percent fall into this category when *amici* are present. This finding indicates that, while the litigants and *amici* attempt to steer the justices toward particular issues with their written legal arguments, the justices rarely even talk about these issues if they are not concerned with them during the oral arguments. The remaining data in table 4.1 bear out this claim. Indeed, in cases without *amicus* participation, 47 percent of all issues discussed during conference are found in both the briefs and in the oral argument transcripts, while 51 percent of the issues discussed during conference fall into this category when *amici curiae* participate.

Table 4.1 also provides compelling evidence that the justices on the Supreme Court gather information from the oral arguments beyond the briefed arguments, and then discuss this information during the initial phase of their coalition formation and opinion-writing processes. Specifically, 45 percent of all issues discussed at conference come directly from the oral arguments (in cases with and without *amicus* participation). This percentage is statistically greater than the issues that are briefed only, and is also greater than

Table 4.1
The Origin of Information Discussed by the
Supreme Court during Conference Discussions

Cases without *Amicus* Participation (N = 45)

Where Information Originates	Number of References
Brief only	22 (5)***
Brief and oral argument	217 (47)
Oral argument only	211 (45)
No matching references	14 (3)***
Total issues discussed at conference	**464 (100)**

Cases with *Amicus* Participation (N = 30)

Where Information Originates	Number of References
Litigant brief only	2 (0)***
Amicus brief only	0 (0)***
Litigant and *amicus* brief	0 (0)***
Litigant brief and oral argument	47 (11)***
Amicus brief and oral argument	26 (6)***
Litigant and *amicus* brief and oral argument	142 (34)
Oral argument only	188 (45)
No matching reference	16 (4)***
Total issues discussed at conference	**421 (100)**

Percentages are in parentheses and are rounded to the nearest whole number.
Note: T-tests are conducted between the mean number of issues discussed during conference that were raised at oral argument only, and each of the other categories.
* = Difference is significant at 0.10 level; ** = Difference is significant at the 0.01 level; *** = Difference is significant at the 0.001 level (two-tailed tests).

the number of issues that are neither briefed nor discussed during the oral arguments (p < .001 for each comparison). However, in cases without *amici* this percentage is statistically indistinguishable from issues that are briefed and raised at oral arguments. Similarly, in cases with *amici*, the number of issues unique to oral arguments is not statistically different from issues raised in the litigant briefs, *amicus* briefs, and oral argument transcripts.[4]

These initial data suggest that—in most cases—the justices do not simply show up for oral arguments and "leave with nothing," as existing anecdotal accounts dictate. Rather, as shown in chapter 2, the justices gather an abundance of information from these proceedings, and then they discuss this information during conference. In other words, during the first post–oral argument discussion of a case (when tentative votes are also taken), information from oral arguments plays a prominent role. This supports the first and second conference hypotheses.

Individual Justices and Conference

Like the findings in Chapter 2, the results in the previous section only allow me to make aggregate claims about how the Supreme Court uses issues discussed during oral arguments. However, unlike the aggregation problem in chapter 3, I can disaggregate the conference data to assess the behavior of individual justices. Indeed, because the justices write down comments made by their colleagues during conference, I can determine the extent to which each justice raises issues from oral arguments.

The results of this individual-level analysis are presented in table 4.2, and they indicate that the justices are quite consistent in the extent to which they individually discuss issues from oral arguments during conference. Column 3 shows that, across the board, justices rarely discuss issues raised in the legal briefs but that garner no attention during oral arguments. Fewer than 5 percent of all issues raised by each justice fall into this category. Additionally, two of the justices—O'Connor and Blackmun—have no conference remarks in this category. Even the three justices with the highest percentage of comments in this category—Powell, Stewart, and Burger—focus only 4 or 5 percent of their comments during conference on these non-orally argued issues.

Column 4 provides further evidence that the information garnered during oral arguments plays an integral role in the Court's decision-making process. It demonstrates that when the litigants or *amici curiae* brief an issue and the Court then discusses the issue during oral arguments, the justices are quite likely to discuss it during conference. Indeed, over 50 percent of all conference arguments fall into this category for five of the ten justices, while three

Table 4.2
References to Orally Argued Issues by
Individual Justices during Conference Discussions

Justice	Total Statements	Issues Unique to Briefs	Briefed and Orally Argued Issues	Issues Unique to Oral Arguments	No References
Marshall	32	1 (3)	16 (50)	15 (47)	0 (0)
Brennan	123	2 (2)	70 (57)	48 (39)	3 (2)
Stevens	68	2 (3)	33 (49)	31 (45)	2 (3)
Stewart	131	5 (4)	64 (49)	55 (42)	7 (5)
White	122	3 (0)	69 (57)	44 (36)	6 (5)
Blackmun	103	0 (0)	54 (52)	44 (43)	5 (5)
Powell	56	3 (5)	21 (38)	32 (57)	0 (0)
O'Connor	18	0 (0)	9 (50)	9 (50)	0 (0)
Burger	151	6 (4)	67 (44)	71 (47)	7 (5)
Rehnquist	81	2 (2)	29 (36)	50 (62)	0 (0)
Totals	885	24 (3)	432 (49)	399 (45)	30 (3)

Note: For this table I have combined the cases with and without *amicus* briefs. Numbers in parentheses are the percentage based on the total arguments raised by a justice during conference. The percentages in the totals row are the percentage of total arguments from each information source.

Data Sources: Comparison of litigant and *amicus* briefs, transcripts of oral arguments, and justices' conference notes.

of the justices have more than 40 percent of their comments in this category. Even the two justices with the fewest comments in column 4—Rehnquist and Powell—make more than a third of their conference arguments about issues that are both briefed and then discussed during oral arguments.

While column 4 suggests justices are generally more likely to consider arguments at conference that are discussed during oral arguments than they are to discuss issues only found in the legal briefs, column 5 demonstrates that oral arguments also play a unique role in the Court's decision-making process. For eight of the justices, more than 40 percent of their conference arguments fall into this category. Additionally, three of the justices make at least 50 percent of their conference arguments focusing on issues in this column.

Overall, table 4.2 provides additional support for the first two conference hypotheses. Specifically, it demonstrates that justices across the ideological spectrum treat orally argued issues in a similar manner during conference discussions. Indeed, none of the justices discuss many issues that are only raised in the litigant or *amicus* briefs. At the same time, they all discuss a large number of issues that were raised by one or more of their colleagues during oral arguments—many of which are raised during these proceedings but not in the legal briefs. Thus, this table offers systematic evidence that oral arguments play a unique informational role in the Supreme Court's decision-making process. It also corroborates the justices' public statements (see chapter 1) that oral arguments are clearly on their minds during conference discussions.

The Strategic Model, Oral Arguments, and Conference

Certainly the aggregate and individual-level data provide support for the first two conference hypotheses. But these analyses do not tell the whole story because they do not indicate the types of information from oral arguments the justices deem important enough to bring to the conference table. Rather, they simply demonstrate the origin of the information discussed during the initial phases of the decision-making process. Additional analysis is necessary, as I argue justices should focus on very specific types of information as strategic actors.

POLICY CONSIDERATIONS. If oral arguments provide unique information that helps justices reach their policy goals, then I expect a majority of the policy arguments discussed at conference should appear in the oral argument transcripts. Additionally, a significant proportion of the conference's focus on policy should be on issues discussed during oral arguments but not in the legal briefs. These claims are born out in table 4.3, where it is apparent that the vast majority of the Court's policy discussions during conference focus on issues addressed by one or more justices during oral arguments.

Even more striking is that less than 1 percent of the Court's policy discussions during conference focus on issues that are found exclusively in the legal briefs or in neither the briefs nor the oral argument transcripts. In other words, almost 100 percent of conference discussion about policy focuses on issues addressed by the Court during oral arguments. Statistically, the difference between the Court's discussion of issues found in both the briefs and the oral argument transcripts, and the first two issues found exclusively in the briefs is significant at the $p < .001$ level in a difference of means test. This is an overwhelmingly important finding because it demonstrates the prominent role oral arguments play as the Court begins its internal deliberations.

Table 4.3
References to Policy during
Supreme Court Conference Discussions (N = 75 Cases)

Where Information Originates	N (References)	Percentage
Brief only	1	0
Brief and oral argument	207	52
Oral argument only	189	48
No matching references	1	0
Total policy issues discussed during conference	398	100

Data Sources: Comparison of litigant briefs, *amicus* briefs, transcripts of oral arguments, and conference notes of Justices Brennan, Powell, and Douglas. I have combined the cases with no *amici* with those where *amici* participate.

To test the the hypothesis that the Court should discuss policy issues unique to the oral arguments, I turn to the third row of table 4.3, which indicates that 48 percent of the Court's policy discussion during conference falls into this category. This is also a significantly greater part of the discussion than policy issues that are only briefed, or that are neither briefed nor raised during oral arguments ($p < .001$).

Several anecdotes provide substantive support of the statistical findings outlined above, and also delineate the different types of policy arguments the justices discuss during conference. In *Gertz v. Robert Welch Inc.* (1974), Justice Powell was concerned about the specific standard the Court should use to decide when a published news story is in the public interest and therefore falls under the *New York Times v. Sullivan* (1964) test.[5] Powell raised this question to Gertz's counsel during the argument:

POWELL: May I ask a question? You made a statement that there was no public or general interest in the representation in the civil suit by Mr. Gertz. Who determines whether or not there is a public interest in a libelous statement?

COUNSEL: "Mr. Justice Powell, I would suppose that the ultimate arbiter as to whether there is or is not public interest must be the courts and, certainly, ultimately, this Court. (transcript of oral argument, 12)

At conference, Brennan's notes indicate that Powell could not agree with the public interest standard proposed by counsel. "Can't accept 'public interest' standard because leaves power to press to determine what is 'public interest'" (Brennan conference notes in *Gertz*, November 14, 1973). In other words, Powell raised the question during oral arguments and then made a point to address this issue at conference.

During conference the justices also refer to questions from oral arguments that may help them formulate beliefs about the state of current public policy, as they did in *Hynes v. Mayor of Oradell* (1976). This case involved a candidate running for public office who wanted to solicit votes and donations door-to-door. Oradell had an ordinance that required anyone soliciting in this manner to provide advance written notice to the local police department before beginning to canvass. Hynes sued, claiming the ordinance should be declared void because it was unclear about what it would take to be in compliance with it. Counsel for the appellant made four constitutional claims, including arguments that the ordinance violated the First and Fourteenth Amendments to the Constitution, that it was void for vagueness, and that it violated the Privileges and Immunities Clause (for coding rules of the briefs, see chapter 2). Counsel for the borough made one main argument, claiming the challenged law provided a "correct balance between the right of the public generally, and the rights of the appellant" (brief for appellee, 2).

Because the appellant focused only on constitutional issues, and because the appellee provided a very general argument, the justices clearly had room to ask questions beyond the written record during the oral arguments.

First, they asked about the requirement that solicitors must provide notice to the police:

COURT: Mr. Major, may I interrupt you at this point? How would you construe the requirement of identification in writing? Would a postcard suffice?

COUNSEL: I would say that it can be done in writing. I would say anything in the way of a driver's license or anything that I am what I pretend to be.

COURT: Your answer suggests that one would have to go to the police station and prove the correctness of his identity. Is that in your thinking?

COUNSEL: The ordinance says "in writing." It does not require a personal appearance at the police station. Now, the only time, I think, that the suggestion you have in mind or the thought that may be troubling you would come into play is if the person were not recognized by his writing. (transcript of oral argument, 25)

Additionally, the justices were concerned with the purpose of the law: preventing crime.

> COURT: Right [a postcard would suffice]. Would you follow up then and discuss for an appropriate period how you think that sort of regulation would prevent crime?
>
> COUNSEL: Definitely not.
>
> COURT: It would not?
>
> COUNSEL: No sir.
>
> COURT: You think the ordinance does not serve the purpose for which it was enacted?
>
> COUNSEL: Definitely. (transcript of oral argument, 26–27)

Exactly how the Court would address these issues was not clear during oral arguments, but the justices did focus on them during conference. Both Powell's and Brennan's notes indicate the chief justice raised both issues. He pointed out, "Ordinance is miserably drawn. But objective is legitimate. State may require pre-registration of persons who solicit door to door. Protection of crime obviously is a legitimate end" (Powell and Brennan, conference notes in *Hynes,* December 12, 1975). In short, these specific issues from the oral arguments found their way into the conference discussions about how the Court should ultimately rule.

Sometimes the justices also express their beliefs about certain policies more adamantly during conference, as Chief Justice Burger's comments in *Memphis Light, Gas, and Water Division v. Craft* (1978) indicate. In this case, the Court had to determine whether a homeowner had a property right to receive electricity from a public utility. The Court asked counsel during oral argument if the property right fell under section 1983 of the 1964 Civil Rights Act. At conference, Brennan recorded that Burger was clearly against the use of this statute. The notation reads, "Use of 1983 is absurd—makes me gag" (Brennan conference notes in *Craft,* November 4, 1977).

Table 4.3 also indicates that policy discussions during conference discussion often focus on information about policy the justices did not or could not obtain from the litigants' briefs. *Montayne v. Haymes* (1976) illustrates this statistical finding. In this case the justices had to determine whether a prison inmate is entitled to a hearing before being moved from one prison to another, even if the transfer is for punitive reasons rather than for disciplinary reasons. As the respondent, it is clear that Haymes had won in the circuit court. However, during oral arguments, Haymes' counsel abandoned the Second Circuit's opinion, which argued the district court had not determined whether Hayme's transfer violated his due process rights under the Fourteenth Amendment. Wasby et al. (1992, 9) note that when counsel take this tack, or more generally make concessions during oral arguments, these arguments are new issues on the record. In this case the justices focused many of their questions during oral arguments on two issues: (1) why the respondent now wanted to disavow a decision in his favor; and (2) what he wanted the Court to do.

This issue clearly played a part in the conference discussion, and the justices explicitly refer to it as "new." Justice Brennan argued, "Counsel for respondent abandoned CA2's opinion, and argues a new issue: that complaint states a denial of right to petition for grievance" (Powell conference notes in *Montayne,* April 23, 1976). Justice Stevens agreed: "Clear on face of hearing that inmate was entitled to a hearing on what we call 'new issue'" (Powell conference notes in *Montayne,* April 23, 1976). Like the analysis in *Roe, Haymes* demonstrates that new issues are raised during oral arguments, and then discussed by the justices at conference.

EXTERNAL ACTORS. The second aspect of the strategic model posits that justices must account for how external actors may react to their decisions. Remember that the Court has no enforcement power and must therefore rely on others to carry out the policy choices that it makes. Additionally, the justices must be cognizant of how Congress may react to their decisions, because Congress has the power to overturn Court decisions with which it disagrees. Thus, the justices must have information about other actors' preferences, as well as about how far they can take a particular policy before there may be a backlash of sorts.[6]

The analysis in chapter 2 suggests that, in accordance with this theory, a key focus for the justices during oral arguments is the preferences of actors beyond the Court. As with the analysis of how the Court deals with policy, these findings have little value if the justices do not discuss and ultimately utilize this information when making substantive decisions. Table 4.4 suggests that, while the justices discuss external actors far less often than they discuss their policy options in a case, when they do raise these issues during conference, the information is almost always discussed during oral arguments and much of it originates during these proceedings.

Eighty-three percent of all references to external actors during conference are discussed during oral arguments but are not addressed in the litigant or *amicus* briefs. Another 12 percent of all references to other actors are discussed during these proceedings even though the legal briefs also addressed them. Combined, this means that 95 percent of all conference discussion

Table 4.4
References to External Actors during
Supreme Court Conference Discussions (*N* = 75 Cases)

Where Information Originates	*N* (References)	Percentage
Brief only	0	0
Brief and oral argument	12	12
Oral argument only	85	83
No matching references	5	5
Total references to external actors during conference	102	100

Data Sources: Comparison of litigant briefs, *amicus* briefs, transcripts of oral arguments, and majority opinion case syllabi. I have combined the cases with no *amici* with those where *amici* participate.

points about external actors are filtered by, or originated during, oral arguments. Further, the justices discuss none of the arguments about external actors that are briefed but not addressed during oral arguments.[7] Finally, only 5 percent of conference discussion about external actors focuses on points found neither in the briefs nor in the oral argument transcripts. Clearly, then, the justices utilize oral arguments to gather information about other actors' beliefs or preferences, and they view this information as important enough to consider as they begin the bargaining and opinion-writing phase of the decision-making process.

Conference discussions throughout the sample support these data. For example, questions about Congress and congressional statutory intent are often on the justices' minds during oral arguments, and then discussed at conference. In *Forsham v. Harris* (1980) the justices sought to determine how Congress interprets the Freedom of Information Act as it applies to researchers who have federal grants. At the end of the respondent's argument, the justices asked several questions about this point:

COURT: Well, the purpose of the federal grant is what Congress determines it to be, isn't it?

COUNSEL: That's correct, Your Honor, but in this case and in the cases of most federal grants, the purpose is to support and to assist these institutions and entities as they pursue their own goals.

COURT: Could Congress make all of these records public records by definition?

COUNSEL: I believe the Congress perhaps could, if it wanted to define agency records to include the records of grantees, I think they could make that definition. In this case they have not. (transcript of oral argument, 47)

Justice Blackmun picked up on this point during conference, and invoked the legislative history, as well as how he thought the problem should be solved. Brennan notes these comments: "Something in legislative history that might say Congress intended to reach grantees—let them say so if they mean to include them" (Brennan conference notes in *Harris*, November 2, 1979). This comment indicates Blackmun is not necessarily thinking about how to interpret the legislative history, but about how the current Congress would interpret the particular FOIA provision. Indeed, his point is that unless Congress now says what it thinks the law means, the Court will interpret it the way the justices see fit. This is consistent with the strategic model, which suggests it is the current Congress about which the justices must be concerned because it is this Congress, rather than the enacting Congress, that can sanction the Court for decisions with which it disagrees (see Eskridge 1991a; Epstein and Knight 1998a).

In other cases, the justices grapple with how to interpret congressional preferences when the intent of a law is unclear. In another FOIA case, *United States v. Weber Aircraft Corp.* (1984), the Court dealt with how this law applied to military personnel involved in tests of aircraft safety. After asking counsel about how the Supreme Court should interpret the meaning of the law, both Chief Justice Burger and Justice Blackmun raised this issue at conference. Burger argued that the *Machin* privilege outlined in the legislative history was "just wrong" (Brennan conference notes in *Weber Aircraft*, January 13, 1984). On the other hand, Blackmun seemed less concerned with the original intent of the law than with what the Court should do in light of the fact that later Congresses never clarified the legislation. Powell notes Blackmun's point that the Court "Ought deal with failure of Congress to clarify, with omission of any reference to *Machin*" (Powell conference notes in *Weber Aircraft*, January 13, 1984). Again, Blackmun's tack seems strategic, as he wants to deal with how the Court should act in light of the fact that Congress never clarified the statute. The point, however, is that the justices do ask about Congress during oral argument, and then address their concerns during conference discussions.

Beyond Congress, the justices discuss other actors at conference. In *Martin v. Ohio* (1987), the Court used oral arguments to ask counsel about other states' policies concerning a self-defense defense for an accused murderer (see chapter 2). At conference, Justice White addressed this point. He argued that this issue would not arise often as "All but 4 states avoid this problem" for these types of cases (Powell conference notes in *Martin,* December 5, 1986). Although White was not explicitly trying to discern others' preferences, his comment suggests that he was looking to the whole picture. That is, he wanted to know how the Court's decision might affect laws in states beyond Ohio. As argued in chapter 2, these types of questions are important for the justices' ability to determine the breadth of their decisions, and ultimately how other actors may react to them.

INSTITUTIONAL RULES. As a final test of the third hypothesis, consider table 4.5. This table demonstrates that over 80 percent of all references to institutional rules during conference are discussed during the oral arguments. Importantly, 60 percent of all issues in this category originate during these proceedings. This suggests that when the Court discusses threshold issues and precedents that may affect their decisions, they garner the vast majority of this information directly from the oral arguments. Additionally, when the legal briefs make threshold arguments or address precedent in their main arguments (that is, beyond simply including a passing reference to a case in the brief), and then the Court seeks to clarify these points during oral arguments, the justices are likely to raise these arguments during conference. Indeed, 22 percent of the Court's references to institutional rules during conference fall into this category.

Table 4.5
References to Institutional Norms and Rules
during Supreme Court Conference Discussions (N = 75 Cases)

Where Information Originates	N(References)	Percentage
Brief only	16	8
Brief and oral argument	45	22
Oral argument only	119	60
No matching references	21	10
Total institutional rules discussed during conference	201	100

Data Sources: Comparison of litigant briefs, *amicus* briefs, transcripts of oral arguments, and majority opinion case syllabi. I have combined the cases with no *amici* with those where *amici* participate.

Altogether, the data presented in this section lead to three main conclusions. First, the Court's discussions at conference include many references to issues that were raised at oral arguments. This indicates that the justices may not be wasting their time with these proceedings, but are gathering information that they then invoke during conference discussions about the merits of a case. As such, this evidence clearly cuts against the conventional wisdom that oral arguments play little role in the justices' decision-making process. Second, much of the information from oral arguments discussed during conference centers on issues that may help the justices make efficacious policy decisions that also satisfy their own goals. That is, the focus is on policy, external actors' preferences, and precedent. This makes the strategic account of oral arguments even more credible because it shows that justices actually utilize the information they gather during oral arguments when making substantive legal and policy decisions.

Finally, and maybe most important, much of the information that comes from oral arguments, which the justices then discuss at conference, clearly originates during these proceedings. This is key evidence because it is the strongest argument against the conventional wisdom, which claims oral arguments matter very little. Indeed, that the justices gather information for the first time during oral arguments suggests that they use these proceedings to obtain the information they believe will help them make efficacious policy choices. The point, then, is that justices do not simply use oral arguments as a symbolic tool to legitimize the Court's existence. Rather, the justices use this time to gather information that will help them make decisions in line with their own preferences.

Is Information from Oral Arguments Discussed during the Opinion-Writing Process?

After conference, the chief justice, or the senior justice in the majority, assigns the majority opinion. Once an opinion is written, it circulates between chambers. During this opinion-writing phase memoranda also circulate between the chambers, either publicly (where each chamber receives a copy) or privately (where memos are sent to a select number of justices). Sometimes memos simply tell the opinion writer that a justice is willing to join the majority or that she will circulate a dissent. These are usually one-line memos that say, "Please join me," or "In due course I will dissent." However, some memoranda are used to discuss, and to bargain over, the substantive choices the justices must make (see e.g., Maltzman, Spriggs, and Wahlbeck 2000; Epstein and Knight 1998a; Wahlbeck, Spriggs, and Maltzman 1996). As such, these memoranda provide another opportunity to discern the informational role that oral arguments play in the Court's decision-making process. If issues raised during these proceedings are subsequently debated during the Court's internal bargaining process, then there is additional evidence that the oral arguments provide information that the justices believe is important for helping them make substantive decisions.

I coded the intra-Court memoranda to determine the total number of references to orally argued issues, as well as to the number of references made to specific issues from these proceedings. While these data are the most difficult in my sample from which to generalize (because the N is so small), they do indicate that information from oral arguments continues to play a role for the Court even after conference.

Across the sample of cases, a total of ninety-nine issues in the memoranda are discussed during the oral arguments. Specifically, intra-Court memoranda cite issues raised during oral arguments an average of 1.3 times per case over the sample (SD = 2.4).[8] Beyond demonstrating that information from oral arguments continues to garner the justices' attention as they craft and circulate their opinions, this finding provides an interesting picture of the Court's decision-making process. That is, when combined with the data from the oral argument transcripts and justices' conference notes, it demonstrates the natural progression of how justices reach substantive decisions in cases they hear. First, litigants and *amici curiae* try to set the boundaries of the case in their briefs (Epstein and Kobylka 1992). Second, during oral arguments, justices raise questions about briefed arguments and also add issues to the record by asking questions about issues beyond the legal briefs. Third, during conference discussions, which occur within a few days of oral arguments, the justices clearly discuss issues raised at these proceedings. Finally, once the majority opinion is assigned and the bargaining and accommodation process begins, the justices concentrate their discussion on those few substantive issues on which the case will ultimately turn (which tend to come out during oral arguments). In short, at each stage of the decision-making process the justices continue to focus the case on fewer and fewer issues and, as they do, oral arguments play a continuous informational role for the justices.

These general data are telling, but do not indicate whether oral arguments provide unique information that the justices discuss during the opinion-writing stage. Thus, I also provide evidence of the extent to which issues raised only at oral arguments are discussed in memoranda. The results are compelling: 37 percent of all references to the oral arguments in the Court's memoranda refer to issues raised during these proceedings, but not in the litigant or *amicus* briefs.

I also analyze the degree to which justices explicitly discuss policy issues from oral arguments in their conference memoranda. Over 40 percent of all the references to oral arguments in memoranda focus on policy issues raised by the justices during these proceedings. Additionally, of the forty-two orally argued policy issues discussed in memoranda, over 21 percent originate during the oral arguments. This means oral arguments clearly provide unique information about the Court's policy options that the justices deem important enough to discuss as they bargain with one another about how to substantively decide a case.

Conclusion

This chapter began with an explanation of how issues from oral arguments found their way into conference deliberations and bargaining memoranda in *Roe v. Wade*. From there I provided systematic and anecdotal evidence that demonstrates how *Roe* is not an anomaly but a phenomenon that occurs in many cases the Supreme Court decides. In chapter 2, Justice Stevens said oral arguments provide a time to raise issues he wants his colleagues to think about. This chapter provides evidence that the justices do think about issues discussed during these proceedings. Indeed, that the justices raise issues from the oral arguments during conference discussions and in memoranda circulated during the opinion-writing process suggests Stevens' account is accurate. The final piece of the puzzle, then, is whether justices ultimately utilize these issues in their final decisions on the merits. This is the focus of the next chapter.

Chapter 5

―――⊰◈⊱―――

Oral Arguments and Decisions on the Merits

Introduction

The discussion of *Roe v. Wade* (1973) in chapters 2 and 4 leads to two conclusions about how Supreme Court justices used information obtained during oral arguments in this case. First, the justices raised at least one issue at these proceedings that was not addressed by the parties in their briefs. To reiterate, the justices inquired about when, if ever, a state's interest in preserving life outweighs a woman's right to choose abortion on demand. Second, the justices discussed this issue at conference and during the opinion-writing process, which suggests the answer to this question continued to play a prominent role in their discussions about how to set policy in this case. The final piece of the puzzle is to determine what the Court ultimately did with this information. Thus, I turn to the majority opinion written by Justice Blackmun. The evidence is compelling. Justice Blackmun raised five main points concerning the Texas abortion law, the third of which centered on the question raised by Justice White during both sessions of oral arguments in *Roe*:

> State criminal abortion laws, like those here, that except from criminality only a life-saving procedure on the mother's behalf without regard to the stage of her pregnancy and other interests, violates Due Process in the 14th Amendment, which protects against state action the right to privacy including a woman's qualified right to terminate her pregnancy. Though the state cannot override that right, it has legitimate interests in protecting both the pregnant woman's health and the potentiality of human life, each of which interests grows and reaches "compelling" at various stages of pregnancy. (Majority Opinion Syllabus, *Roe v. Wade*)

In other words, after the discussions with his colleagues (see chapter 4), Blackmun settled on the trimester scheme to demarcate the various stages of abortion rights. While this doctrine became the cornerstone of abortion rights in America, I am more interested in the fact that this issue was not briefed by the parties (Roe's attorney admitted as much during oral arguments), but still wound up playing a definitive role in the Court's final policy choice. This account of *Roe*, and other examples I could cite, demonstrate the Supreme Court can and does decide issues based on information gleaned uniquely from oral arguments.

The first half of this chapter uses systematic data to assess whether the Court's reliance on oral arguments in *Roe* represents a more general practice on the Court. This analysis directly tests the conventional wisdom (Segal and Spaeth 1993, 2002; Rohde and Spaeth 1976) that oral arguments play little, if any, role in how the justices decide cases that they hear. By focusing on the substantive arguments in a case, rather than on the dispositive votes cast by the justices, I will be able to draw direct links between these proceedings and the Court's ultimate decisions—something that scholars thus far have been unable to accomplish.

I proceed as in the previous chapters by explicating the hypotheses and methods I will use to test them. From there I present the results of how, and the extent to which, the Court rules on issues from oral arguments in its majority opinions. If I can show that the justices consistently rule on issues discussed during these proceedings, then there is support for the idea that oral arguments play a key informational role in the Court's decision-making process.

It might be adequate to stop at this point in the analysis, but demonstrating that justices actually use information from oral arguments when making substantive decisions raises a related, and equally important, question. That is, when are the oral arguments most likely to come into play as the justices seek to set legal policy? Indeed, if justices are strategic actors who care about placing policy close to their preferred outcomes, then understanding when they will use this tactic is important as well. To answer this question, then, I determine the conditions under which the Court is most likely to turn to these proceedings for information when making decisions. Theoretically, I argue that justices are more likely to utilize information from the oral arguments when the substantive outcome of a case is uncertain, in spite of the information they already possess (i.e., from litigant and *amicus curiae* briefs). To test this theory, I invoke data beyond those utilized in the rest of the book. Specifically, I analyze all formally decided cases with signed opinions (i.e., signed opinions from orally argued cases) from the Vinson, Warren, and Burger Courts (1946–1985). With all of this information combined, this chapter provides a compelling picture of how the Supreme Court utilizes oral arguments in its opinions, and the conditions under which it is likely to do so.

Oral Arguments and Supreme Court Opinions

Beyond finding that justices discuss precedent when deliberating about how to decide a case, Knight and Epstein (1996) also argue, "Perhaps the most important evidence of a norm of *stare decisis* comes in the way the Court treats existing precedent. If the justices consistently and often overturned principles established in past cases, then we could hardly label *stare decisis* a norm—in the sense that norms establish expectations about future behavior" (1029). In short, the simple fact that the Court uses precedent in its opinions demonstrates the importance of *stare decisis*. A similar logic applies to the Court's reliance on oral arguments. While I do not expect the justices to invoke issues discussed during these proceedings as often Epstein and Knight find they invoke precedent, the fact that they would do so at all demonstrates the informational role oral arguments play in the Court's decision-making process. Thus, in line with Knight and Epstein's argument about precedent, I hypothesize the following:

Opinion Hypothesis 1: If oral arguments play a significant informational role in how the Court makes substantive decisions, then a significant proportion of the issues that the justices rule on in their majority opinions should address issues discussed during oral arguments.

In testing this hypothesis, there are two ways the justices could use oral arguments to gather information. As Justice Rehnquist wrote in chapter 1, these proceedings can help the Court clarify arguments forwarded in the legal briefs. Second, as the data in chapter 2 demonstrate, oral arguments allow the justices to add new issues to the record of a case. The problem is that if the justices only cite issues outlined in the briefs and subsequently discussed during oral arguments, then, although I can claim that oral arguments play a role in how the Court decides cases, I cannot argue that these proceedings play a unique informational role in this process. Indeed, evidence supporting the first hypothesis is an important step toward demonstrating that the justices do not simply ignore oral arguments when making decisions, but, standing alone, this evidence leaves me with a problem of behavioral equivalence. That is, just as in chapter 2, this evidence does not tell me where the justices obtain the arguments they cite in their opinions. Thus, I must also provide evidence that they rule on issues raised during oral arguments but that the litigant or *amicus curiae* briefs did not address in writing. As such I slightly alter the first hypothesis and also posit that:

Opinion Hypothesis 2: If the oral arguments play a *unique* informational role for the Court, then a significant proportion of all references

to these proceedings in the Court's majority opinions should reference issues raised by the justices during the oral arguments but that the litigants and *amici curiae* did not address in their briefs.

As a final test of the role oral arguments play for the Court, I turn back to the general theory forwarded in this book—the strategic account of decision making (see chapter 1). In accord with this theory, I posit that the justices' predominant focus should be on policy outcomes, how other actors might react to their decisions, and institutional norms and rules that may impede their ability to reach certain decisions. More explicitly, if oral arguments play a unique role in helping the justices shape their preferred goals, I hypothesize the following:

Opinion Hypothesis 3: When deciding policy issues, focusing on external actors' preferences, and invoking institutional rules, the majority of these arguments should be discussed during oral arguments, and a significant proportion should originate uniquely during these proceedings.

Data and Coding Rules

To test the above hypotheses, I compare the briefed arguments (both litigant and *amicus*) and the oral argument transcripts with the majority opinion syllabi for the seventy-five cases in my sample.[1] I employ the same coding scheme utilized in chapters 2 and 4 to differentiate the types of issues the Court addresses in its opinions (see table 2.1). To determine where these issues originate, I use the following decision rules. First, if an issue in the majority opinion syllabus is found in the oral argument transcripts, but not in the briefs, then I code this as a reference to a unique issue from the oral arguments. Second, issues found in the legal briefs but not in the oral argument transcripts are coded as unique issues from the briefs. Third, if an argument is in both the briefs (litigant, *amicus*, or litigant and *amicus*) and in the oral argument transcripts, I code this as a briefed and orally argued issue. By distinguishing between issues found only in the oral argument transcripts and those found there and in the briefs, I can easily overcome the problem of behavioral equivalence discussed in the previous section.

A comparison of the questions the Court raises during oral arguments with its majority opinions should give me a good means by which to determine the ultimate informational role these proceedings play in the justices' decision-making process. If they generally cite, and rule on, issues from oral arguments in their opinions, then there is evidence these proceedings play an integral informational role for how the Court makes decisions on the merits.

Results

In *United States v. 12 200-Foot Reels of Film* (1973), the Court had to decide whether the United States could constitutionally prohibit the importation of obscene material, which the importer claims is for private, personal use and possession only. In his oral argument notes, taken during these proceedings, Justice Powell noted that the solicitor general's "Argument was helpful, especially as summary of prior law—read transcript" (Powell oral argument notes, November 6, 1972). Similarly, in *EPA v. Mink* (1973), Powell wrote that it was an "Excellent argument," and that he should "use transcript if I write" (Powell oral argument notes, November 9, 1972).[2] Although he did not do so in every case, Powell clearly had a penchant for examining the oral argument transcripts, especially if he was going to write the Court's majority opinion.[3]

Powell's behavior suggests that oral arguments can, and sometimes do, play a key role in determining how the Court makes substantive decisions on the merits. To test whether this is the case generally, I initially present descriptive statistics that address this question. In my sample of cases, when *amici curiae* do not participate, the majority opinion cites issues discussed during oral arguments an average of 3.27 times per case (N = 147 citations in 45 cases; SD = 1.70), while in cases with *amici curiae* the majority does so 3.10 times per case (N = 92 citations in 30 cases; SD = 1.28). This means that, even in cases one standard deviation below the mean, the Court still cites more than one issue from the oral arguments per case.[4] More compelling is the fact that 76 percent of all the majority opinion syllabus points (in cases with and without *amici curiae*) focus on issues discussed during the oral arguments. This is a significantly greater number of citations than the Court makes to arguments that are found only in litigant or *amicus* briefs (p < .001 for cases with and without *amici*). When combined with the conference data from chapter 4—recall that on average the justices discuss about eleven issues from oral arguments during conference—these findings demonstrate that the justices continue to focus on oral arguments when writing opinions. As with Knight and Epstein's (1996) analysis of precedent, this is strong evidence that oral arguments play an integral informational role in the Court's decision-making process.

Aggregate Court Behavior

Although these results support my first hypothesis, they allow me to make only limited conclusions. Indeed, with the data presented above it is impossible to determine whether the Court uses oral arguments as a unique source of information. In other words, this initial support for the first hypothesis does not solve the dilemma of behavioral equivalence. Thus, additional analysis is necessary. I do so by determining from where each syllabus point originates. The results are presented in table 5.1.

This table paints a compelling picture. I first turn to issues raised in the legal briefs but not discussed during oral arguments. In cases without *amicus* participation (the top half of the table) only 11 percent of all syllabus points address arguments that are briefed but not discussed during oral arguments. When *amici* participate (lower half of the table), just 6 percent of the majority's main arguments address issues raised only in the litigants' briefs, none refer to issues raised only in *amicus* briefs, and 12 percent address issues found in both the litigant and *amicus* briefs but not in the oral argument transcripts. The implication of this finding is that even though the litigants and *amici* try to set the boundaries of a case with their briefed arguments, the justices are unlikely to rule on issues that enter the record only through the legal briefs. More generally, this speaks to the broader issue of how legal change occurs on the Court (see e.g., Epstein and Kobylka 1992; Wahlbeck 1998).

I next turn to the justices' focus on information outlined in the litigant or *amicus* briefs that is subsequently addressed by the justices during oral arguments. When *amici* do not participate, 44 percent of all syllabus points fall into this category, while this amount increases to 52 percent when *amici* file in a case. This indicates that when the parties or *amici curiae* highlight a point in their briefs and then the justices ask about it during oral arguments, the majority opinion is more likely to address this issue than if the issue is only raised in the legal briefs. Statistically, the difference between these categories is significant ($p < .001$ for cases with and without *amici*). But again, the causation arrow for this relationship is difficult to draw; I still cannot determine whether the Court ruled on these issues because they were briefed by the litigants or *amicus curiae*, because they were discussed during oral arguments, or because the issues were briefed *and then* discussed during these proceedings.

Fortunately, table 5.1 also allows me to determine whether the Court rules on issues discussed during the oral arguments but that are not explicated in the legal briefs. In cases without *amicus* participation, fully one-third of all the majority opinion syllabus points fall into this category, while 24 percent of syllabus points are in this category when *amici* participate. In a difference of means test, the Court is significantly more likely to rule on issues from this category than on those it obtains from the briefs only ($p < .001$ for both sets of cases). However, the Court's propensity to rule on issues unique to oral arguments is statistically indistinguishable from the number of syllabus points that focus on issues found in the briefs and the oral argument transcripts.[5]

Table 5.1
The Origin of Information in Supreme Court Majority Opinions

Cases without *Amicus* Participation ($N = 45$)

Where Information Originates	Number of References
Brief only	22 (11)***
Brief and oral argument	84 (44)
Oral argument only	63 (33)
No matching references	23 (12)***
Total issues in syllabus	**192 (100)**

Cases with *Amicus* Participation ($N = 30$)

Where Information Originates	Number of References
Litigant brief only	7 (6)***
Amicus brief only	0 (0)***
Litigant and *amicus* brief	14 (12)
Litigant brief and oral argument	16 (13)
Amicus brief and oral argument	5 (4)**
Litigant and *amicus* brief and oral argument	42 (35)
Oral argument only	29 (24)
No matching reference	7 (6)***
Total Issues in Syllabi	**120 (100)**

Percentages are in parentheses and are rounded to the nearest whole number.
Note: T-tests are conducted between the mean number of issues in the majority opinions that were raised at oral argument only, and each of the other categories.
* = Difference is significant at 0.10 level; ** = Difference is significant at the 0.01 level; *** = Difference is significant at the 0.001 level (two-tailed tests).

Individual Justice's Behavior

The implication of these results is that oral arguments provide an independent source of information the Court ultimately uses when making substantive decisions on the merits. As the first hypothesis indicates, however, I am also interested in determining whether this finding applies to only a few justices (such as Justice Powell), or whether all of the justices act in a similar fashion. If only one or two justices use these proceedings to gather information, then I cannot conclude that the Court as a whole systematically makes use of information from oral arguments when making substantive policy decisions. Ultimately, this would call into question my general argument about the informational role of these proceedings. On the other hand, if little variation exists among justices, then there is even stronger support for my hypothesis.

Table 5.2 presents the results of this analysis.[6] With only a few exceptions, the justices are consistent in the degree to which they utilize oral arguments in their opinions.[7] First, column 4 indicates that the greatest amount of variation is found in the extent to which each justice cites arguments found only in a litigant or *amicus* brief. Of the ten justices in the sample, only three wrote opinions where more than 20 percent of the syllabus point originated exclusively in the briefs—O'Connor (21 percent), Stewart (44 percent), and Blackmun (35 percent). More telling is that for five justices (Marshall, Stevens, White, Burger, and Rehnquist), less than 10 percent of the syllabus points refer to arguments found in the legal briefs but that were not discussed during oral arguments. Of these five, Marshall and Stevens cite no issues from this category, and Rehnquist cites only one. This suggests that while some justices do rely more heavily on the briefed arguments, most of the justices do not rule on issues discussed in the legal briefs when they are not at least clarified by the Court during oral arguments.[8]

The most consistent behavior across justices is their reliance on issues outlined in the briefs and subsequently discussed during oral arguments (column 5). With the exception of O'Connor (29 percent), at least one-third of all syllabus points in each justice's opinions specifically reference issues in this category. Again, there is some variation—33 percent for Stevens' opinions, and almost 60 percent in Rehnquist's. However, it is clear that, across individual opinions, the justices in this sample rely on issues raised by the parties, but only if the justices also discuss these issues during oral arguments.

Finally, I consider the category that allows me to test the extent to which each justice relies on issues unique to oral arguments when writing majority opinions. These results are found in column 6 of table 5.2. With only three exceptions, the justices are consistent in their tendency to invoke issues found in

Table 5.2
References to Orally Argued Issues by Majority Opinion Writer

Opinion Writer	Written Opinions	Total Arguments in Syllabus	Issues Unique to Briefs	Briefed and Orally Argued Issues	Issues Unique to Oral Arguments	No References
Marshall	2	4	0 (0)	2 (50)	2 (50)	0 (0)
Brennan	5	16	3 (19)	6 (37)	3 (19)	4 (25)
Stevens	4	14	0 (0)	7 (50)	7 (50)	0 (0)
Stewart	3	9	4 (45)	3 (33)	2 (22)	0 (0)
White	10	38	2 (5)	21 (55)	12 (32)	3 (8)
Blackmun	6	34	12 (35)	18 (53)	2 (6)	2 (6)
Powell	16	76	14 (18)	33 (44)	23 (30)	6 (8)
O'Connor	2	14	3 (21)	4 (29)	6 (43)	1 (7)
Burger	16	71	4 (6)	33 (46)	24 (34)	10 (14)
Rehnquist	9	32	1 (3)	19 (59)	10 (31)	2 (6)
Totals	73	308	43 (14)	146 (47)	91 (30)	28 (9)

Note: Numbers in parentheses are the percentage based on total arguments raised by the opinion writer. Second, only seventy-three cases are used for this table as two cases had no majority opinion. One, *Parker Seal Co. v. Cummins* (1976), was decided by an equally divided Court, and the other, *Poelker v. Doe* (1977) was decided by a *per curiam* decision.

Data Sources: Comparison of litigant briefs, transcripts of oral arguments, and syllabi of Supreme Court opinions found in U.S. Reports or the Howe database (*United States Supreme Court Reports* 1996).

the oral argument transcripts but not in the briefs. For each of the other seven justices, over 30 percent of all syllabus points reference arguments in this category. This reinforces the notion that, while issues raised only during oral arguments do not command a majority of any one justice's substantive decisions, they do play a significant role for all of them.

The Strategic Model, Oral Arguments, and Supreme Court Opinions

The above findings suggest individual justices, and the Court as a whole, are most likely to rule on issues raised in legal briefs and then discussed during oral arguments. This clearly supports the first hypothesis. At the same time, I find strong support for the hypothesis that a significant proportion of the issues upon which the Court rules originate during these proceedings. My final task in this section is to test the third hypothesis—in issue areas that help the justices act strategically, the majority of information should be discussed only during oral arguments, and a significant proportion of these issues should be discussed only during these proceedings.

POLICY CONSIDERATIONS. I initially seek to determine from where the Court draws its information about policy. If oral arguments truly provide unique information that helps justices reach their policy goals, then I expect a majority of the policy arguments made in majority opinions to be discussed during oral arguments. Additionally, as hypothesis 3 predicts, a significant proportion of the arguments should be discussed during oral arguments but not in the briefs. These claims are borne out in table 5.3, where it is apparent that the Court draws its policy arguments from the briefs and oral arguments in about the same proportions as it does information more generally. Initially, then, this table provides support for the first two hypotheses in this chapter. More important, this table also provides support for the third hypothesis. While less than 14 percent of the Court's policy arguments stem from arguments in the briefs alone, 61 percent of the syllabus points that focus on policy issues are briefed *and then* discussed by the Court during oral arguments. Statistically, the difference between the Court's reliance on these categories for information is significant at the $p < .001$ level in a difference of means test.

To test the second part of the third hypothesis, I turn to the third row of table 5.3, which indicates that over 25 percent of the Court's syllabus points that focus on policy fall into this category. These results provide even more convincing evidence of the unique role oral arguments play in the Court's decision-making process. Indeed, scholars argue that policy is the most important consideration for the justices (Maltzman, Spriggs, and Wahlbeck 2000; Epstein

Table 5.3
References to Policy in Supreme Court Majority Opinions (*N* = 75 Cases)

Where Information Originates	*N* (References)	Percentage
Brief only	20	14
Brief and oral argument	88	61
Oral argument only	37	25
Total policy issues in syllabi	**145**	**100**

Data Sources: Comparison of litigant briefs, *amicus* briefs, transcripts of oral arguments, and majority opinion case syllabi. I have combined the cases with no *amici* present with those where *amici* participate.

and Knight 1998a; Segal and Spaeth 1993). Combined with the fact that a significant minority of policy arguments in the opinions comes directly from oral arguments, this is strong evidence that these proceedings play an integral informational role in how the Court makes decisions on the merits.

To better understand these findings, and to demonstrate their qualitative impact, I provide two examples of how the Court utilizes oral arguments when making policy decisions. Consider, first, a case where the Court explicitly used information that entered the record only because of a question posed by the justices during the oral arguments. In *Erznoznick v. City of Jacksonville* (1975) the Court considered whether films containing nudity could be shown at a drive-in theatre. Here the justices clearly used oral arguments to form beliefs about the policy set out in the Jacksonville city ordinance. Specifically, they were concerned with the key aim of the policy and asked about it on two levels: whether the ordinance was meant to protect children, and whether it was intended to prevent potential traffic problems around the theater. Neither of these specific issues was addressed in the major arguments of the briefs.[9] The line of questioning concerning protection of children went as follows:

COURT: You don't think children are interested in watching R rated movies?

COUNSEL: I think the children go in that want to see it, you know, they get their parents' permission, they get in a car and they go in. But that's beside the point.

COURT: It is beside the point, because I mean where the parents say, "Don't go to that theater," and then the child says, "I won't go to the theater to see it," and he just goes to the corner and looks for free.

COURT: And that's part of what this ordinance is aimed at . . .

COUNSEL: But if he was looking—

COURT: Isn't this part of what this ordinance is aimed at? (transcript of oral argument, 14–15)

The traffic question was raised earlier on in the appellant's argument.

COURT: Why wouldn't it be a perfectly good ordinance regulating traffic safety? You do not want people driving down the street looking at movies.

COUNSEL: Well, if it were related to traffic safety, then—well, it wouldn't be unless it was so construed. If by its very language it says, "It shall be unlawful to exhibit on an outdoor screen from a public place, a movie."

COURT: Yes, visible from any public street, any movie.

COUNSEL: Well, I think you would have to show that there is some relationship between—

COURT: Wouldn't there be a rational relationship.

COUNSEL: I don't think so. Unless you said where the exhibition is visible from a traveled highway and there is a showing—

COURT: Generally public streets are traveled, aren't they? (transcript of oral argument, 5–6)

Both of these arguments were discussed at conference, and they comprise the second and third syllabus points in Justice Powell's majority opinion:

Nor can the ordinance be justified as an exercise of the city's police power for protection of children against viewing the films. Even assuming that such is its purpose, the restriction is broader than permissible since it is not directed against sexually explicit nudity otherwise limited. (opinion syllabus in *Erznoznick v. Jacksonville*)

Similarly, Powell was unwilling to accept traffic safety as a rational reason for the policy to stay intact.

Nor can the ordinance be justified as a traffic regulation. If this were its purpose, it would be invalid as a strikingly under-inclusive legislative classification since it singles out movies containing nudity from all other movies that might distract a passing motorist. (opinion syllabus in *Erznoznick v. Jacksonville*)

The Court's willingness to explore these policy issues, which were not specifically identified in the briefs, indicates that the justices gained additional information from oral arguments before they felt they could make a policy choice
about the validity of the city ordinance.

The justices also use oral arguments to clarify the basis on which they
should rule before making final policy choices. In *Zacchini v. Scripps Howard
Broadcasting Co.* (1977) the Court was asked to interpret Ohio law as applied to
a First Amendment case.[10] To do so, the justices first had to interpret the specific policy decision of the Ohio Supreme Court. Given that Zacchini's arguments rested on the syllabus of the state court's opinion, the justices needed to
be sure that the syllabus held the weight of law in Ohio.[11] As such, the following exchange took place during the oral arguments:

> COURT: We have been told a good many times in Ohio cases when they
> come here that the law of the case is the syllabus, the head note, not the
> opinion. Is that binding on—is that the law of Ohio?
>
> COUNSEL: Yes, it is, your Honor.
>
> COURT: Now, is that particular concept of Ohio law binding on this
> Court in a First Amendment case?
>
> COUNSEL: I don't think so. I think that this Court must look behind the
> bare syllabus, the three paragraphs that summarize what happened and
> determine what the facts were.
>
> COURT: Well, we have accepted it tacitly I think as binding for some
> purposes . . . (transcript of oral argument, 5–6)

In his opinion, Justice White's first main point is, "It appears from the
Ohio Supreme Court's opinion syllabus (which is to be looked to for the rule of
law in the case), as clarified by the opinion itself, that the judgment below did not
rest on an adequate and independent state ground but rested solely on federal
grounds" (opinion syllabus in *Zacchini*). While this may seem like a minor point,
it supports my argument that, when the justices believe they do not have enough
information about how to make a particular policy choice, they will utilize oral
arguments to gather the necessary information that will help them do so.

EXTERNAL ACTORS. The analysis in chapters 2 and 4 suggests that one of the
Court's key focuses during oral arguments is to gather information about other
actors' preferences. As with the analysis of how the Court deals with policy,
these findings have little value if the Court does not use this information in its
opinions. While table 5.4 suggests that the Court does not often explicitly

Table 5.4
References to External Actors
in Supreme Court Majority Opinions (N = 75 Cases)

Where Information Is Found	N (References)	Percentage
Brief only	2	6
Brief and oral argument	8	25
Oral argument only	22	69
Total references to external actors in syllabi	32	100

Data Sources: Comparison of litigant briefs, *amicus* briefs, transcripts of oral arguments, and majority opinion case syllabi. I have combined the cases with no *amici* present with those where *amici* participate.

address external actors in its majority opinion arguments, when it does so, these issues almost always originate during oral arguments.

This table demonstrates that almost 69 percent of all references to external actors are discussed during oral arguments and not in the litigant or *amicus* briefs. An additional 25 percent are discussed during these proceedings even though the legal briefs also address the issues. Clearly, then, the justices utilize oral arguments to gather information about other actors' beliefs or preferences, and they ultimately use this information in their majority opinions.

Several cases illustrate how the Court uses oral arguments to learn about external actors' preferences. In *United States v. Albertini* (1985), the Court had to decide whether a citizen banned from entering a military base may reenter that base after a certain period without permission of the commanding officer.[12] The justices were concerned with the intent of the law in question as well as with the government's position in the case. Several times during oral arguments, they raised this issue to counsel for the United States. First, they asked what the government's position was:

> COUNSEL: I think the limitation on the duration of a bar letter is found not in section 1382, but in the requirement that administrative actions be reasonable. And therefore, a bar letter cannot extend beyond a reasonable time, and that is the limitation.

> COURT: Do you have any idea what the government's position is on a reasonable time?

COUNSEL: I think it would necessarily depend on circumstances of each case. (transcript of oral arguments, 7)

The justices were also concerned with the congressional intent of the law.[13]

COURT: What does the legislative history show the reasons that the Congress enacted the law? What was the abuse that it called for? I am sure it was not demonstrations or entering the base on open house.

COUNSEL: It was not demonstrations, and Mr. Albertini did not receive his bar letter for demonstrating. The abuse was—

COURT: Why did Congress enact it?

COUNSEL: The legislative history is fairly clear. The problem was that people would come onto bases for various bad—

COURT: To recruit soldiers for prostitution?

COUNSEL: For prostitution, for saloons.

COURT: That was the reason, wasn't it?

COUNSEL: That's right. That's right. And they would be thrown off base, and then before you knew it, they would be back on the base. And Congress had to implement some way to enforce, wanted to implement some way to enforce the commanding officer's warning. (transcript of oral argument, 22–23)

These questions suggest the justices wanted to determine where to place policy in light of the preferences of Congress and the present administration. In her opinion, Justice O'Connor addressed both of these concerns. She pointed out that:

Viewed in light of the ordinary meaning of the statutory language, respondent violated § 1382 when he reentered Hickam in 1981. Moreover, § 1382's legislative history and its purpose of protecting Government property in relation to the national defense support the statute's application to respondent. There is no merit to respondent's contentions that § 1382 does not allow indefinite exclusion from a military base, but instead applies only to reentry that occurs with some "reasonable" period of time after a person's election. (opinion syllabus in *U.S. v. Albertini*)

Even though O'Connor did not refer explicitly to the will of the current Congress, her discussion suggests that the Court consented to the wishes of both the administration and Congress. In short, the Court was cognizant of what the other two branches wanted, and made it clear in its opinion that it supported those views.

The focus on external actors is also exemplified by *Regan v. Taxation with Representation of Washington* (1983). In this case, the Court was faced with deciding whether veterans' organizations, which lobby Congress, should be afforded tax-exempt status when other tax-exempt organizations are not permitted to lobby. One justice used oral arguments to address the point that Congress has always treated veterans' organizations differently than other non-profit organizations.

> COURT: What if Congress instead of giving the veterans organizations a break in the tax statute had simply appropriated $5 million to each of them? Do you think that would be changeable in Court at all?
>
> COUNSEL: I do not.
>
> COURT: This really is not much different.
>
> COUNSEL: I think it is not very much different. I think this Court has made that very clear, and it brings into play another body of doctrine that is also determinative in this case.
>
> COURT: Has not the Congress over a period of years granted a great many benefits to veterans?
>
> COUNSEL: Precisely. (transcript of oral argument, 11)

In his majority opinion, Justice Rehnquist was explicit about what the Court thought of Congress's role in this area. It was not irrational for Congress to decide that tax-exempt organizations such as Taxation with Representation should not further benefit at the expense of taxpayers at large by obtaining a further subsidy for lobbying. Nor was it irrational for Congress to decide that, even though it will not subsidize lobbying by charities generally, it will subsidize lobbying by veterans' organizations. Thus, the majority indicated that it had considered Congress's preferences quite relevant in this case, and in the end ruled in line with Congress—one of the most important external actors the Court has to face.

Along with specific references to external actors, the Court also seeks information about the implications of a case (see chapter 2 for an explanation of why these questions also help the justices learn about external actors). In *Ward v. Illinois* (1977) the Court was faced with the task of interpreting the obscenity standards set out in *Miller v. California* (1973). During the state of Illinois's oral argument, the Court asked how far the state believed it could push its standards:

COURT: My second question is: Presume the state statute says our state legislature shall prohibit everything in the examples given in *Miller*, and also sadism and masochism, and give four or five other specific concrete examples, and then says: And in addition, anything which is patently offensive and as the general standard of—in other words, it has the general category and it lists the specifics as examples that the *Miller* opinion dealt with. Would that satisfy *Miller* do you think?

COUNSEL: I think it would, Your Honor. I would think that would go—

COURT: In other words, all you need is an example, you don't need any limitation? (transcript of oral argument, 29)

Invoking the crux of this line of questioning, Justice White's opinion argued that:

> Sado-masochistic materials are the kind of materials that may be proscribed by law, even though they were not expressly included within the examples of the kinds of sexually explicit representations that *Miller* used to explicate the aspect of its obscenity definition dealing with patently offensive depictions of specifically defined sexual conduct. (opinion syllabus in *Ward v. Illinois*)

INSTITUTIONAL RULES. As a final test of the third hypothesis, table 5.5 demonstrates that over 50 percent of all references to institutional rules in majority opinions are discussed during oral arguments but were not delineated in

Table 5.5
References to Institutional Norms and Rules in Supreme Court Majority Opinions ($N = 75$ Cases)

Where Information Is Found	N (References)	Percentage
Brief only	4	10
Brief and oral argument	15	37
Oral argument only	22	53
Total institutional arguments in syllabi	**41**	**100**

Data Sources: Comparison of litigant briefs, *amicus* briefs, transcripts of oral arguments, and majority opinion case syllabi. I have combined the cases with no *amici* present with those where *amici* participate.

the litigant or *amicus* briefs. Combined with the fact that more than 36 percent of the Court's references to institutions were briefed and then discussed during the oral arguments, it is evident that when the justices raise questions about precedent or threshold issues during oral arguments, they are likely to address these issues in their opinions.

This limited focus on institutional rules is seen in *Turner v. Safley* (1987), where the Court focused on the constitutionality of a state ban on prisoner-to-prisoner correspondence within the Missouri penitentiary system (see chapter 2). During the respondent's oral arguments, one justice focused on which precedent best fit the case at hand:

> COURT: Well, is *Martinez* the closest case to you or not?
>
> COUNSEL: Yes, sir, it is. *Martinez* is clearly the closest.
>
> COURT: Why isn't *Jones* a more appropriate standard in this case for the inmate to inmate correspondence, just as it was for the inmate to inmate meetings.
>
> COUNSEL: Well, there are—there is some—
>
> COUNSEL: *Martinez* had to do with the rights of non-inmates, really. And I wonder whether *Jones* does not provide the appropriate test? (transcript of oral argument, 46)

Justice O'Connor took issue with the respondent's analysis. Her first point was clear about this: "The lower courts erred in ruling that *Procunier v. Martinez* (1974) and its progeny require the application of a strict scrutiny standard of review for resolving respondents' constitutional complaints" (majority opinion syllabus in *Safley*). The point is that *Martinez* was raised by one of O'Connor's colleagues during the oral arguments, and she ultimately utilized the analysis that came to light during these proceedings in her opinion.

Along with using oral arguments to clarify precedents, the Court also uses information about threshold issues gathered during these proceedings. In *Bender v. Williamsport Area School District* (1986), a student religious group (Petros) sued the school district because the district would not permit the organization to meet at the school. The district lost in the court of appeals, and a single school board member took the case to the Supreme Court. The justices were unsure whether the man (Youngman) even had standing to argue before the Court. They brought this issue out during oral arguments at several points, but two exchanges most vividly highlight their concern. First, during the discussion with the petitioner's attorney:

COURT: So, he could have been a plaintiff in the case originally?

COUNSEL: Yes, Your Honor. That is our view of the *McCollum* case.

COURT: So you think he is still in the case? (transcript of oral argument, 7–8)

The justices also raised this point with Youngman's own attorney

COURT: So, you think that here he is now a respondent?

COUNSEL: That is right.

COURT: And, that in his capacity as a member of—in his official capacity of—

COUNSEL: That is right. That is in his official capacity.

COURT: And, he can speak for the entire board? (transcript of oral argument, 26–27)

In line with these questions, Justice Stevens made it clear in the Court's opinion that Youngman had no standing in the case. As such, the majority claimed the court of appeals had no jurisdiction to hear the case, and they vacated and remanded the decision. Specifically, Stevens wrote that even though Youngman was a board member, this position did not permit him to "step into the shoes of the Board" and invoke its right to appeal (majority opinion syllabus in *Bender*). Additionally, he wrote, "Nor did respondent have standing to appeal in his capacity as a parent of a student attending the high school." In short, the Court actually dismissed this case using a threshold issue that was not explicitly briefed, but that was addressed by the justices during oral arguments. While this tactic is not used often, the Court does at times obtain such information from the oral arguments, and then use it to dismiss or remand a case based on procedural grounds.

Overall, this section provides compelling evidence about how, and the extent to which, the Supreme Court uses information garnered from oral arguments in its opinions. The findings comport with Wasby et al.'s (1992) analysis that, in its *per curiam* opinions, the Supreme Court often invokes information from oral arguments. As they note, "The Court's *per curiam* opinions provide clear evidence that oral argument at times—but certainly not always—has been directly relevant to the Court's disposition of a case—and at times determinative of the outcome" (30). What neither my results nor Wasby et al.'s results demonstrate is exactly when the justices are likely to utilize information from these proceedings in their opinions. This is an important phenomenon to analyze because to fully understand how strategic justices utilize oral arguments to reach certain outcomes, we must also understand when they are likely to turn to these proceedings for information that will help them do so. Without such an analysis, the findings in chapters 2 through 5 would be incomplete.

When Will the Court Actually Use Information from Oral Arguments?

To determine when the Court is most likely to use information from oral arguments in its opinions, I make two additional assumptions about judicial decision making beyond the general strategic theory outlined in chapter 2. First, as I argued in chapter 3, most Supreme Court justices possess some degree of uncertainty about the final policy that will be set by the majority coalition. Second, because justices often face uncertainty, they must gather information about their full range of policy options, to help them form beliefs about other actors' preferences, and to assess institutional barriers that may keep them from making decisions close to their preferred outcome. Also as noted in chapter 1, justices can gather this information from a variety of sources: litigant briefs (Epstein and Kobylka 1992), *amicus* briefs (Spriggs and Wahlbeck 1997), and the media (Epstein and Knight 1998a). There are times, however, when the information provided by these sources does not help the justices reach their preferred goals. Thus, they will have to find additional information that will help them do so. As the first four chapters demonstrate, oral arguments provide an important opportunity to obtain such information.

More specifically, I argue that if justices are not strategic actors, if case outcomes are known with certainty after conference, and if justices have all the information they need from the written briefs, then there would be little reason for them to use oral arguments to elicit additional information when crafting opinions. However, if case outcomes are less than certain after conference, and if the written briefs do not provide all the information they need, then we might expect justices to actually need information from oral arguments when crafting policy decisions. Thus, I view oral arguments as a final opportunity for justices to gather information that will lead them to their desired outcome. In other words, when the information from litigant and *amicus* briefs fails to help a justice push a case toward her preferred outcome, she may turn to oral arguments for additional information that may help her do so.

Hypotheses

Based on the assumptions outlined above, I argue that the level of uncertainty surrounding a case leads the majority opinion writer to look beyond the litigant and *amicus* briefs to obtain information that may help the majority coalesce around a given policy choice. This uncertainty may emanate from two key sources: the stability of the majority conference coalition, and specific case characteristics.

Majority Coalition Stability

Initially I test five hypotheses that focus on how uncertainty about the stability and cohesiveness of the conference majority coalition affects an opinion writer's decision to utilize information from oral arguments. First, when a majority coalition is ideologically heterogeneous there is more uncertainty about the policy outcomes that will emerge from it than from a coalition that is homogenous (Maltzman, Spriggs, and Wahlbeck 2000). Thus, the more heterogeneous a coalition, the more difficult it should be for those in the coalition to agree on a particular outcome. As such, when the coalition is ideologically heterogeneous I expect the members of the coalition to seek additional information. Specifically, I hypothesize the following:

> **Majority Coalition Distance Hypothesis: Opinion authors writing on behalf of an ideologically heterogeneous coalition will be more likely to seek information from oral arguments to help the coalition members agree on a policy outcome.**

Second, when justices switch from one coalition to another, they not only create uncertainty about the makeup of the potential majority coalition, but they create uncertainty about the policy that will eventually emerge in the majority opinion. Indeed, a justice presumably changes votes because the other side has accommodated his views about a case, or because he has been persuaded that he initially joined the wrong coalition (Maltzman and Wahlbeck 1996a). When this happens, the majority opinion author should be more likely to seek additional information to keep his coalition intact. This leads me to predict the following:

> **Voting Fluidity Hypothesis: As the number of justices with fluid votes increases in a case, the opinion author is more likely to utilize issues raised from oral arguments in his opinion.**

Third, justices who are nearer to the center of the Court are more likely than ideologically extreme justices to waver between the majority and minority views in a case (Hoekstra and Johnson 2003). I am particularly interested in cases when the median justice writes the opinion for the Court. In these cases, she may need to look beyond the legal briefs for information that will convince her to stay with the majority rather than to defect to the minority coalition. One tactic she can use to bring the coalition together in this circumstance is to utilize information from oral arguments. Additionally, because she is the most moderate justice, when the median writes the majority opinion, she may need to find additional arguments to prevent the more extreme coalition members from defecting.[14] Therefore, in contrast to other justices, I expect:

Median Justice Hypothesis: When the median writes for the majority coalition, she is more likely to turn to oral arguments for information to keep the coalition together.

Fourth, in my sample of cases, the majority opinion author changes (between conference and the time a final decision is rendered) in about 5 percent of the cases. I argue that, while not a common occurrence, a change in majority opinion authorship after conference also increases the level of uncertainty about the legal and policy outcomes that will ensue (Hoekstra and Johnson 2003). First, if an assignment is changed to a justice who initially authored a dissent, that justice still needs four colleagues to agree with his draft opinion. As a result, he may have to alter the substance of that opinion to keep the newly formed majority intact. While I may not expect wholesale legal or policy changes, it is likely substantive changes will be needed to secure the new coalition. Additionally, switching authors based on an initially mistaken assignment also creates uncertainty—especially if the author changes from an extreme justice to a more moderate justice (or vice versa). Thus, I argue that authorship changes increase uncertainty about the eventual outcome of a case and the new author may need additional information to keep the coalition together. This leads me to expect:

Authorship Change Variable: When an opinion is reassigned after the initial assignment is made at conference, the majority is more likely to cite oral arguments in its opinion.

Finally, when a case is particularly salient, the justices' views are more frequently fixed and intensely held, which means that they are more likely to hold fast to their policy positions stated at conference.[15] Past research indicates, however, that this leads justices to bargain more frequently before ultimately joining an opinion coalition (Spriggs, Maltzman, and Wahlbeck 1999). This bargaining, in turn, increases doubts about the policy outcome of that case. Moreover, in salient cases, the justices may fear the extra scrutiny the majority opinion is likely to receive once the Court's decision is announced. This is precisely what happened in *Immigration and Naturalization Service v. Chadha* (1983). In his conference notes, Justice Powell captures Chief Justice Burger's fear that the legislative veto "is highly sensitive politically. Wish we could avoid the issue." Of course, the Court eventually had to hand down a decision, but only after the case was held over for reargument. After the conference vote finally held the veto unconstitutional, Burger sent around his opinion drafts (six in all) with a note saying that the issue was likely to attract "microscopic—and not always sympathetic!—scrutiny from across the park [that is, in Congress]" (quoted in Epstein and Walker 1998a, 254). For the foregoing reasons, I expect:

Case Salience Hypothesis: The Court is more likely to use information from the oral arguments in its opinions in politically and legally salient cases.

Case Characteristics

Beyond the coalition stability variables, specific case characteristics may also lead to uncertainty about case outcomes. For instance, when a case involves multiple legal dimensions, justices may turn to oral arguments if they do not have enough information from the briefs to determine which dimension controls. Consistent with this argument is the finding that justices change votes after conference in cases involving multiple issues or legal provisions (Maltzman and Wahlbeck 1996a). Two other measures may also indicate case complexity. The number of separate opinions in a case may serve as an indicator of increased case complexity, because as the number of drafts being circulated between chambers increases, uncertainty about the ultimate policy the majority opinion will announce increases. Finally, Hoekstra and Johnson (2003) argue that the Court often reargues cases with complex legal and policy issues. Thus, I posit the following hypotheses regarding complex cases:

Case Dimensions Hypothesis: The majority is more likely to turn to the oral arguments in cases with multiple issues or that implicate multiple laws than in cases that only cover one legal or issue dimension.

Number of Separate Opinions: Cases that generate more opinions indicate greater policy uncertainty and thus should be associated with higher rates of citation to orally argued issues.

Reargument Hypothesis: When the Court hears additional oral arguments in a case, the majority is more likely to utilize issues from oral arguments in its opinions.

Data and Methods

To test the above hypotheses, I invoke data sources beyond the sample of cases used in the rest of the book. First, I created a data set that includes every formally decided case, with a signed opinion, from 1946 to 1985 by merging Spaeth's (2001a) *Expanded Supreme Court Database* with his *Burger Court Judicial Database* (2001b). These databases provide information about conference votes, final votes, opinion writers, and case complexity (among others). To supplement these data, a research assistant analyzed each of these opinions from the *United States Supreme Court Reports* (1996) to determine the extent to which the Court cited oral arguments in its majority opinions.[16] The search was conducted using the Howe electronic database and was done with a Boolean search of the phrase "oral argument."[17] Table 5.6 delineates the number of citations to oral arguments in majority opinions between 1946 and 1968. Clearly, the Court uses this tactic in fewer than 10 percent of all cases.[18]

I employ two dependent measures to determine when the Court is likely to use information from the oral arguments. The first is a count of the total references to these proceedings in the Court's majority opinion for each case.[19] The problem with this measure is that it does not distinguish whether an issue is discussed during oral arguments and in a litigant or *amicus* brief, or whether

Table 5.6
Total References to Oral Arguments in Majority Opinions
for All Formally Decided Cases

Number of Cites per Case	Frequency (Cases)	Percentage of Cases
0	4,382	90.9
1	356	7.4
2	67	1.4
3	10	0.2
4	3	0.1
5	1	0.0
Total	4,819	100.0

Source: Data obtained from Spaeth's (1999) *Expanded Supreme Court database*, and the *Burger Court Database* (Spaeth 2001). The sample includes all formally decided cases that include a signed opinion from 1946 to 1985.

it was only discussed during oral arguments. As such, while these results can support my hypotheses, I again face a potential problem of behavioral equivalence. Given this problem, I test the hypotheses on a second dependent variable based on a subset of the first measure—a count of references to issues discussed during oral arguments but not in the legal briefs. This measure distinguishes between issues when the opinion author writes, "counsel made this point in their briefs and at oral arguments," and when he explicitly argues that, "this point was raised during oral arguments." Because the justices make this distinction themselves, I assume the latter phrase is a citation to an issue discussed only during the oral arguments, while the former is also delineated in the legal briefs. Although this is not a perfect solution, I am confident it will allow me to determine whether oral arguments play a unique role in the Court's decision-making process.

Because both of the dependent measures are discrete, I cannot use traditional linear regression to model this phenomenon (see chapter 3). As Long (1997, 217) points out, "The use of linear regression models for count outcomes can result in inefficient, inconsistent, and biased estimates." There may be many reasonable alternative models, but because there are an abundance of zeros in the data, I employ the same model—a negative binomial regression as I did in chapter 3.

The model contains several independent variables, and table 5.7 provides summary statistics for them, as well as for the two dependent measures. To test the hypotheses about uncertainty created by coalition instability, I include the following variables: (1) the standard deviation of the majority coalition's issue-specific ideology for each case;[20] (2) the number of justices with fluid votes between conference and the final merits vote;[21] (3) whether the issue-specific median justice writes the opinion; and (4) whether, after conference, an opinion is reassigned to a new author.[22] To measure political salience, I use Epstein and Segal's (2000) dichotomous variable that measures whether an account of the case appeared on the front page of the *New York Times* (Epstein and Segal 2000). Finally, to measure legal salience, I code all cases where the Court struck down a law as unconstitutional as 1, and all others 0 (see Maltzman, Spriggs, and Wahlbeck 2000).

To capture uncertainty caused by case complexity, I use three measures. First, I include a general measure of a case's legal dimensions that is coded 1 for all cases that have either multiple legal provisions or multiple issue areas, and 0 otherwise. Second, I count the total number of opinions authored in a case from Spaeth (2001a, 2001b). Third, I determine which cases are slated for reargument (Hoekstra and Johnson 2003). Cases in this category are coded 1, and 0 otherwise.

Table 5.7
**Variables Affecting the Court's Propensity to
Cite Oral Arguments (N = 4,819)**

Variable	Mean	Min	Max	SD	Hypothesized Direction
Dependent Variables					
Total cites to oral arguments by majority	0.12	0.00	5.00	0.40	
Cites to unique oral argument issues in majority	0.11	0.00	5.00	0.39	
Independent Variables					
Coalition heterogeneity	15.25	0.21	37.69	6.19	+
Number of justices with fluid votes	0.94	0.00	9.00	1.45	+
Median justice opinion writer	0.11	0.00	1.00	0.31	+
Authorship change	0.05	0.00	1.00	0.22	+
Case dimensions	0.26	0.00	1.00	0.44	+
Number of opinions circulated in case	2.55	1.00	8.00	1.19	+
Case is reargued	0.03	0.00	1.00	0.18	+
Legal salience	0.05	0.00	1.00	0.21	+
Political salience	0.16	0.00	1.00	0.37	+

Results

Tables 5.8 and 5.9 present the results of the analysis.[23] While the results are slightly different between tables, they paint a clear picture of when the Court will turn to oral arguments in making its decisions. In the first model, three of the coalition uncertainty variables help explain when the Court is likely to cite any issues from the oral arguments.[24] In the second model, coalition heterogeneity and the median justice opinion writer variable help explain when the Court will cite issues unique to these proceedings.

Table 5.8
Negative Binomial Regression Estimates for the Court's Propensity to Cite Issues Raised during Oral Arguments in Its Majority Opinions

Variables	Coefficient	Robust Standard Error	Significance (One-Tailed Test)	Correct Direction?
Constant	−3.81	0.17	0.00	
Coalition heterogeneity	0.05	0.01	0.00	Yes
Number of justices with fluid votes	0.06	0.03	0.04	No
Median justice opinion writer	0.23	0.14	0.06	Yes
Authorship change	0.09	0.20	0.32	Yes
Legal salience	0.16	0.21	0.22	Yes
Political salience	−0.15	0.13	0.13	No
Case dimensions	0.26	0.11	0.01	Yes
Number of opinions circulated in case	0.25	0.04	0.00	Yes
Case is reargued	0.05	0.25	0.41	Yes
α (alpha)[a]	2.58	0.39	0.00	
N	4,819			
Wald χ^2 (9 d.f.)	109.06		0.00	

a The alpha coefficient provides a test of whether the negative binomial or the Poisson is the appropriate modeling choice (see note 11 for an explanation). One-tailed tests are used because I have explicit directional hypotheses (Blalock 1979).

It is intuitive that the coalition heterogeneity variable has an effect in both models because under this condition the opinion writer will have a more difficult time keeping the coalition together. As a result, he may have to look beyond the legal briefs for information that will create common ground between those in the coalition, and oral argument transcripts provide a good place to do so. Additionally, the median justice is more likely than any of the other justices to cite orally argued issues. Like Justice Blackmun in *Roe v. Wade* (1973), the median often has the job of bringing a coalition together, and this

Table 5.9

Negative Binomial Regression Estimates for the Court's Propensity to Cite Issues Raised *Only* during Oral Arguments* in Its Majority Opinions

Variables	Coefficient	Robust Standard Error	Significance (One-Tailed Test)	Correct Direction?
Constant	−3.88	0.18	0.00	
Coalition heterogeneity	0.05	0.01	0.00	Yes
Number of justices with fluid votes	0.04	0.03	0.13	Yes
Median justice opinion writer	0.21	0.15	0.08	Yes
Authorship change	0.12	0.20	0.26	Yes
Legal salience	0.12	0.22	0.29	Yes
Political salience	−0.20	0.14	0.08	No
Case dimensions	0.20	0.11	0.04	Yes
Number of opinions circulated in case	0.26	0.04	0.00	Yes
Case is reargued	−0.09	0.27	0.36	No
α (alpha)[a]	2.69	0.43	0.00	
N	4,819			
Wald χ^2 (9 d.f.)	99.56		0.00	

* By *only* raised at oral arguments, I mean issues that were addressed during these proceedings but *not* in the litigant or *amicus* briefs.

a The alpha coefficient provides a test of whether the negative binomial or the Poisson is the appropriate modeling choice (see note 11 for an explanation). One-tailed tests are used because I have explicit directional hypotheses (Blalock 1979).

finding suggests that one way he can do so is by turning to information from oral arguments. The model in table 5.8 also suggests that when more justices exhibit voting fluidity during the opinion-writing process, the author may need to find information beyond the legal briefs to keep the coalition intact. Finally, there is only scant evidence that case salience affects the Court's propensity to cite oral arguments in its majority opinions. In the model that seeks to explain any references to these proceedings, neither of the salience variables reaches statistical significance. However, when a case is politically salient, the Court is slightly more likely to cite issues that are discussed during oral arguments but not in the legal briefs.

Both models also confirm that when a case is highly complex, the justices are more likely to turn to oral arguments for information that will help them make policy choices. While the reargument variable does not reach statistical significance in either model, both the case dimension variable and the measure of how many opinions are written in a case increase the likelihood that the Court will take this tack. The implication is that the justices need more information in complex cases and a pertinent source of such information is oral arguments.

Beyond the statistical effects, these models have clear substantive effects. I evaluate these effects separately for each model by calculating predicted probabilities. When all the independent variables in table 5.8 (which predicts any cites to oral arguments) are held at their sample mean or modal values, the probability that the Court will cite oral arguments in its majority opinion is 9 percent. From this baseline, I determine predicted probabilities for the statistically significant variables while holding the others constant. When the coalition is ideologically heterogeneous (SD = 37.69), the probability increases to 25 percent, while it decreases to 4 percent when the heterogeneity is at its lowest (SD = 0.21). The other clear effect comes from the number of opinions written in a case. When this variable is at its maximum (nine opinions), the likelihood of a reference to oral arguments is 38 percent, while it decreases to 6 percent when only one opinion is written in the case. On their own, neither the issue complexity variable, the median justice variable, nor the fluidity variable exhibit significant substantive effects.

Combinations of the statistically significant variables show even stronger effects. When coalition heterogeneity is at its maximum and nine opinions are written in a case, the probability that the majority opinion will cite oral arguments is 76 percent. When these conditions hold and the fluidity variable is set at its maximum (nine vote switches), the probability jumps to 90 percent. It increases another 5 percent when the median writes. Finally, if all of these conditions hold and the issue dimension variable is set at 1, the probability reaches a stunning 98 percent! That is, when uncertainty about the ultimate outcome of a case is close to its maximum, the majority opinion writer is almost certain to turn to oral arguments for information about how to decide the case.

I derive similar results from the model that seeks to predict when the Court will cite issues that only enter the record because they were discussed during oral arguments. When all the independent variables in table 5.9 are held at their sample mean or modal values, the probability that the Court will cite oral arguments in its majority opinion is 8.5 percent. When the coalition is ideologically heterogeneous (SD = 37.69), the probability increases to 24 percent, while it decreases to 4 percent when the heterogeneity is at its lowest (SD = 0.21). The other effect comes from the number of opinions written in a case. When this variable is at its maximum (nine opinions), the likelihood of a reference to oral arguments is 31 percent, while it decreases to 6 percent when only one opinion is written in a case. Again, on their own, neither the issue dimension variable, the median justice variable, nor the fluidity variable exhibit significant substantive effects.

Combinations of the statistically significant variables lead to smaller yet still very strong effects. When coalition heterogeneity is at its maximum and the nine opinions are written in a case, the probability that the majority opinion will cite oral arguments is 68 percent. When these conditions hold and the fluidity variable is set at its maximum, the probability jumps to 79 percent. It increases another 6 percent when the median writes. Finally, if all of these conditions hold and the issue dimension variable is set at 1, the probability increases to 90 percent.

Conclusion

This chapter provides the ultimate evidence that oral arguments can—and do—play a significant informational role for how Supreme Court justices make substantive legal and policy decisions. Initially, I showed that on average the Court cites issues discussed during oral arguments more than three times per case. More important, I demonstrated that almost one-third of all references to oral arguments were made to issues discussed during those proceedings but not in the written legal briefs. This is a key distinction because it suggests, in many ways, that the oral arguments in a case provide unique information the justices use when they make substantive choices about the merits of a case.

The second section provides evidence that, while the Court does not often turn to oral arguments when making substantive decisions, it does so under one key condition: when the outcome of a case is in doubt. Based on the statistical and substantive findings from this analysis, I am able to make claims about when justices are likely to exhibit this behavior and show that there are conditions under which the Court is almost guaranteed to use oral arguments in its opinions.

These findings directly challenge the conventional assumption (see e.g., Rohde and Spaeth 1976; Segal and Spaeth 1993, 2002) that oral arguments play little if any role in how Supreme Court justices decide. If these proceedings were little more than a time for the Court to demonstrate that it does consider arguments or for the justices to display that not everything they do is highly secretive, then I would not have found such dramatic results. In fact, I probably would have found very little support for my hypotheses. However, in line with what the justices themselves say about oral arguments (see chapter 1), it is clear that these proceedings play a key informational role for them as they make legal and policy decisions.

Ultimately, these findings concur with the research of Maltzman, Spriggs, and Wahlbeck (2000), Epstein and Knight (1998a), and Caldeira, Wright, and Zorn (1999), who persuasively argue that scholars should pay greater attention to how policy develops on the Court, rather than simply paying attention to the final votes on the merits. Indeed, just as these scholars document how the deliberative process affects the Court's policy choices (e.g., the agenda-setting stage; opinion assignment; opinion writing), I also seek to explain how justices pursue policy goals in a collective environment and under a given set of formal and informal rules. In other words, while oral arguments are themselves interesting I am also interested in these proceedings for what they can tell us about the nature of the deliberative processes on the Court. The insights in this chapter add to the growing body of literature showing that the justices are engaged in a "collegial" endeavor and do not act, as previously thought, like nine separate law firms (Maltzman, Spriggs, and Wahlbeck 2000).

Chapter 6

❧❦❧

Conclusions and Implications

Introduction

D aniel Webster was perhaps the greatest advocate ever to appear before the Supreme Court and, as it did in the *Dartmouth* case, his oratory often won the day. Even though few questions were asked during the oral arguments in Webster's era, his arguments in this case epitomize why these proceedings play a central role in the Court's decision-making process: Webster presented the Marshall Court with policy arguments as well as with arguments about the implications of the case. This behavior comports with the major theme in this book—namely that oral arguments provide information to justices that allows them to act strategically. In this final chapter I consider these key findings, and then turn to the implications of this research. Finally, I make some general comments about what these findings mean for the debate about the Court as a countermajoritarian institution in the American democracy.

Oral Arguments and Supreme Court Decision Making

The analysis throughout this book demonstrates that justices use oral arguments to seek information about their policy options, other actors' preferences, and institutional rules that may constrain their ability to make certain decisions. In the aggregate, justices devote over 40 percent of all their questions during oral arguments to policy considerations. Although limited in scope, the individual-level results support the aggregate findings by demonstrating that, across the ideological spectrum, justices are predominantly focused on policy during these proceedings. Beyond policy considerations, the Court focuses on external actors' preferences. Indeed, more than one-third of all questions asked during oral arguments focus on the preferences of actors beyond the Court. Together with questions about policy, it is clear that the justices use these proceedings to determine exactly where they can place policy in light of other actors' preferences.

As strategic actors, I also hypothesize that justices should raise new issues during oral arguments. That is, they should delve into areas not entered into the case record by the litigant or *amicus* briefs. The evidence supporting this hypothesis is overwhelming. Almost 80 percent of all the justices' questions refer to arguments that were not raised in these briefs. For specific issues, over 70 percent of policy questions are new, over 95 percent of questions about external actors are new, and almost 80 percent of all questions about institutional rules are new. This is compelling evidence that Supreme Court justices use oral arguments to gain information beyond the briefs that they believe will help them make decisions in line with their preferred goals.

There is also convincing evidence that oral arguments begin the coalition formation process as the justices move toward final decisions. While I cannot generalize beyond Justice Powell's behavior, the data certainly support my hypotheses about how I expected him to use these proceedings. That is, he listened to his colleagues' questions—especially those who would most likely help him secure majority coalitions. I also substantiated the link between Justice Powell's behavior and the resulting coalitions during the Court's opinion-writing process. This finding has strong implications for how game theorists understand the role of signaling, cheap talk, and information gathering as political actors try to form coalitions. At the same time, it demonstrates to judicial scholars that, contrary to the attitudinal model, Supreme Court justices do consider their colleagues' preferences when making decisions.

Chapter 4 provides the first empirical evidence to date that justices consider information from the oral arguments as they begin to decide the substantive legal and policy issues of a case. The most persuasive evidence that these proceedings play a role in the Court's decision-making process is that more than 90 percent of all the justices' comments during conference refer to issues that were discussed during oral arguments. Even more important is the fact that well over 40 percent of all issues discussed at conference entered the record for the first time during these proceedings. The justices also discuss orally argued issues in memoranda sent between chambers during the opinion-writing process. Indeed, over the sample, at least one issue from the oral arguments is raised in the memoranda per case. This figure is bolstered by the fact that 37 percent of all references to oral arguments in memoranda refer to issues raised during these proceedings, but that were not raised in the litigant or *amicus* briefs. In short, a significant minority of issues that the justices discuss as they bargain over substantive outcomes are issues that the Court discusses during oral arguments.

The most compelling evidence is found in chapter 5. While the previous chapters show that justices gather information during oral arguments and discuss this information in their meetings thereafter, the ultimate test is whether this information is used in the Court's final opinions. These data tell a profound story. Almost 30 percent of all the legal and policy points made in majority opinion syllabi refer to issues that the opinion writer obtained directly from the oral arguments. In addition, almost 50 percent of all issues in the syllabi refer to information found in both the briefs and in the oral argument transcripts.

The results for the specific issue areas are also telling. Well over 80 percent of all policy issues in the majority opinion syllabi refer to issues raised during the oral arguments. The results are similar for references to external actors' preferences and institutional rules. Indeed, 94 percent of references to external actors and 90 percent of references to institutional rules were discussed during the oral arguments. This suggests that much of the information that can help the justices make decisions is discussed during the oral arguments, and oftentimes comes directly from what transpires during these proceedings.

Implications for Understanding Supreme Court Decision Making

A survey administered to federal appellate and trial court judges indicates that 100 percent of these judges would limit oral arguments to fifteen or twenty minutes, and 90 percent would choose to eliminate these proceedings altogether (Rehnquist 1984, 1015, citing a Federal Judicial Center survey). More than half of the judges surveyed also argued that most attorneys can write briefs that are so effective that oral arguments are unnecessary. It seems, then, that many federal judges agree with the conventional wisdom in judicial politics that oral arguments play little role in how cases are decided. These results would be disturbing to the many Supreme Court justices who posit that oral arguments play a vital role in their decision-making process (see chapter 1). They are also disturbing in light of the findings presented throughout this book, which have clear implications for decision making on the U.S. Supreme Court as well as on lower federal and state courts.

For the academy, the findings here fill several voids in the literature about Supreme Court decision making. Most generally, scholars possess little systematic understanding about what transpires during oral arguments in the Supreme Court. Most information regarding this decisional stage is derived from journalistic accounts (Woodward and Armstrong 1979) and from writings by the justices (Rehnquist 2001) or former clerks (Lazarus 1999). Additionally, the scholarly studies that touch upon oral arguments largely consist of analyses in single cases, or in only a few cases (e.g., Benoit 1989; Cohen 1978; Wasby, D'Amato, and Metrailer 1976). Further, while scholars continue to focus on almost every other aspect of the Court's decision-making process, we have largely ignored the oral arguments. This is no longer a viable research strategy. The results presented here suggest the information justices obtain from these proceedings serves a purpose much greater than scholars have yet realized.

Third, the analysis demonstrates that Supreme Court justices do seek information beyond that which enters the record in the written briefs filed by the parties and *amici curiae*. Specifically, my results clearly demonstrate that oral arguments provide the perfect time for justices to add issues to the legal record that were not included in the briefs. This, then, means that the oral arguments are an invaluable and unique tool for the justices because, unlike the information they receive from litigants, *amici curiae*, or other outside sources, they can use these proceedings to force the attorneys to provide information that they themselves want.

A fourth implication of this research focuses on the assumption, made by many scholars of the separation of powers (Martin 1996, 1997, and 2001 are exceptions), that justices have complete and perfect information about the preferences of the legislative and executive branches (Eskridge 1991a, 1991b; Gely and Spiller 1990; Ferejohn and Weingast 1992). In contrast, my findings point out that justices may not have complete and perfect information—if they did, then I would not have expected them to ask questions about the other branches during oral arguments. At the same time, oral arguments provide a key mechanism for the justices to obtain information about legislative and executive preferences in cases when such information is not readily available.

Finally, this account adds credence to Epstein and Kobylka's (1992, 302) admonition that "the law and legal arguments grounded in law matter, and they matter dearly," as well as to Kassop's (1993) argument that each aspect of the Court's decision-making process must be understood in order to fully comprehend how the justices arrive at their substantive legal and policy decisions. In stark contrast to the attitudinal model, these existing works, combined with my own findings, suggest that Supreme Court justices need more than the confluence of case facts and their policy preferences to make decisions. Rather, they look for answers to substantive legal and policy issues, and then use this information when making decisions.

I do not deny the power of the attitudinal model, nor do I take issue with the fact that justices often vote their own preferences when deciding cases. What I do argue, however, is that there is more that affects justices' final deci-

sions on the merits than simply their personal policy preferences. Some scholars suggest that behind-the-scenes bargaining affects votes (Maltzman,
Spriggs, and Wahlbeck 2000), while others demonstrate that actors beyond the
Court affect how justices act (Eskridge 1991a). In line with these studies, I
demonstrate that the oral arguments must be accounted for when seeking an
explanation for how justices make decisions on the merits. This is consistent
with more general criticisms of the attitudinal model that focus on the fact that
it excludes any intervening explanation for how justices act. As Knight (1994,
6) points out, "the attitudinal model fails to account for factors that may com-
plicate the relationship between an individual justice's vote and the effectuation
of a particular outcome."

Beyond providing the first evidence about the effect oral arguments have
on how justices decides cases they hear, this study teaches a more important
and general lesson about social scientific research. As chapter 1 indicates, scholars have summarily discounted the role of oral arguments but have failed to justify their claims—which makes them suspect. My point is that if scholars are to
make such broad claims—such as insinuating that an entire aspect of the
Supreme Court's decision-making process has no bearing on how decisions are
made—they need to put these claims to the test. Segal and Spaeth (1993, 2002)
fail to do so, and all but a few Court scholars have also ignored this process. If
we are to fully understand how justices make decisions, we must no longer fail
to include this part of the process in our explanations and accounts of how the
Supreme Court reaches decisions on the legal and policy merits of a case.

Overall, then, this research should significantly and unequivocally change
the way Supreme Court scholars study how justices make decisions. Indeed,
scholars must now be cognizant of the fact that the only public aspect of the
Court's decision-making process plays a role in how the justices decide cases. Of
course, evaluating the more precise role that these proceedings play is difficult,
but it is certain that they play a critical informational role in the justices' examination of their policy options and their assessment of external actors' preferences. In the end, the analyses presented in chapters 2 through 5 demonstrate
that the conventional wisdom can no longer stand as the predominant view of
oral arguments. In short, oral arguments play a continuous and prominent role
in how the United States Supreme Court makes decisions on the merits of cases.

Future Research

Despite the compelling systematic evidence presented throughout this book,
there is much more for scholars to analyze in this area of the Court's decision-
making process. In terms of focus on issues specific to the Supreme Court,

there are several fruitful avenues for future scholarship. For instance, Galanter (1974) argues that repeat players are more successful before the Supreme Court, while McGuire (1993a, 1993b) provides evidence that attorney experience is the key to success. Given the high level of advocacy displayed by some of the nation's top attorneys throughout the history of the Court—from Daniel Webster to Thurgood Marshall—it would be interesting and beneficial to determine whether these factors also play a role in the extent to which oral arguments affect the Court's decisions. Given that the analysis in chapter 2 is conducted only at the aggregate level, it is also important that future research focus on additional individual-level analysis. The anecdotal findings presented there, as well as those offered by McFeeley and Ault (1979) and Benoit (1989) suggest that variation does exist in how individual justices utilize these proceedings as they gather information about a case, but further systematic analysis is warranted because the existing findings focus on only a few justices. One more specific line of inquiry about individual justices may concentrate on whether moderate or so-called swing justices (e.g., Justices O'Connor and Kennedy) use oral arguments more often, and to a greater extent, than justices who are more ideologically extreme (e.g., Justices Scalia and Stevens).

The data on *amicus curiae* participation raise an additional area of future inquiry. Spriggs and Wahlbeck (1997) demonstrate that the Court is likely to utilize information provided by *amicus* briefs in its opinions. Conducting a similar analysis that includes the information from the oral arguments as well as from the briefs would shed additional light on the role that *amici* play in the Court's decision-making process. Finally, the analysis here should lead scholars to analyze the role of oral communication in other institutions of government. For instance, scholars may want to examine how members of Congress use congressional testimony during floor debate as well as in the final versions of bills presented for votes. Similar analysis could be conducted on agency hearings at the federal government level as well as on hearings at school boards and other committees at all levels of government. In the end, the findings here only scratch the surface on what we can learn from analyzing the Supreme Court's oral arguments. The field is wide open for further inquiry into these and many other areas.

Oral Arguments, the Supreme Court, and the Democratic Process

Since *Marbury v. Madison* (1803), legal scholars have debated the proper role of the Supreme Court in American democracy (Bickel 1962; Tushnet 1985; Ackerman 1984; Seidman 1988; Chemerinsky 1989; Horwitz 1993). This debate continues to confound legal scholars. For instance, Ackerman (1984, 1016) argues that, "Hardly a year goes by without some learned professor announcing that he has discovered the final solution to the countermajoritarian difficulty, or, even more darkly, that the countermajoritarian difficulty is insoluble." Chemerinsky (1989, 71) agrees, as he points out, "Most constitutional scholars for the past quarter-century . . . have seen the task of constitutional theory as defining a role for the Court that is consistent with majoritarian principles." Additionally, Horwitz (1993) suggests that the countermajoritarian dilemma has been the central focus of legal theorists for some time: "The competing conceptions of democracy and its relationship to judicial review . . . have framed the central debates in American constitutional theory during the past fifty years" (62).

More specifically, scholars who debate about the proper role of the Court fall into two camps. One side argues that it is often inappropriate for the Court to make decisions that affect the most important and controversial issues in the United States because justices are unelected and therefore unaccountable to any constituency. As such, the Court poses a "countermajoritarian difficulty" (Bickel 1962). Supporters of this view include Bickel (1962) and Bork (1990), as well as Justice Frankfurter. Others argue that this is precisely the reason the Court exists. That is, because of the problems that often ensue in a democracy—tyranny of the majority being a major concern—the Court acts as a check because it is not accountable to any constituency. Supporters of this side include Chief Justice Warren and Justices Brennan, Marshall, and Fortas (Horwitz, 1993). The two sides of this debate are adamant about their positions, and there is little or no common ground; the Court is viewed either as the quintessential antidemocratic institution or as an appropriate check on the other branches of government.

The theory I forward here, however, combined with the empirical evidence that demonstrates how justices use oral arguments, should lead scholars to understand that common ground can and does exist between the two sides of the countermajoritarian debate. In the past decade, Court scholars have clearly demonstrated that justices account for the preferences of Congress and the executive branch as well as how these institutions may react to their decisions (Marks 1989; Gely and Spiller 1990; Eskridge 1991a, 1991b; Ferejohn and Weingast 1992; Cameron 1993; Martin 1997; Johnson 2003). They do so because both of the other federal branches can punish the Court if the justices run too far afield from where Congress or the executive want policy. Thus, these separation of powers analyses suggest that the Supreme Court does not have complete discretion and therefore the fact that justices are not accountable to any constituency may not do any major harm to our democratic structure.

Whereas the theory about the Court's relationship with the other branches suggests that the countermajoritarian dilemma may not be a dilemma at all, the specific findings I present throughout this book provide empirical support for this theory. Indeed, Supreme Court justices use oral arguments to raise questions about the preferences of political institutions, public opinion, and the impact of their decisions. The point is that while the Court decides cases largely outside of the public eye, the one public aspect of its decision-making process suggests that, even though the justices are technically unaccountable to actors beyond the Marble Palace, they take seriously the idea that they do not make decisions in a vacuum. Rather, there is clear evidence that the justices consider, discuss, and ultimately account for the Court's place in the federal system of government. This should quell fears that the Supreme Court has moved from being the least dangerous branch to being the most powerful, the most unaccountable, and the most antidemocratic branch of the federal government.

Appendix 1:
Data Selection

Data and Case Selection

Data are drawn from several sources. The main sources are litigant and *amicus curiae* briefs, the transcripts of oral arguments, the private papers of justices Powell, Brennan, and Douglas, and the syllabi (summaries) of Supreme Court majority decisions.

Seventy-five cases were randomly selected using the Spaeth (2003) database, with docket number as the unit of analysis. I limited the universe of cases to those decided between 1972 and 1986 because some of the main data sources I employ come from Justice Powell's oral argument notes, his conference notes, and intra-Court memoranda found in his case files. Since these were the years that he sat on the bench, it is logical to limit the sample to these years for the purposes of comparison and reliability.

Coding Rules

Written Briefs

I coded the principal points in the "Argument" section of the outline at the beginning of each brief. This accords with Supreme Court Rule 24.6, which says that: briefs must be "logically arranged with proper headings" (Stern, Gressman, and Shapiro 1993, 548). Litigants and *amici* therefore use headings at the beginning of their briefs so that the reader knows exactly what they will argue in the remainder of the brief. The principal argument is defined as the Roman numeral headings in the outline. If these headings were too vague (e.g., "Law X violates the First Amendment"), then I coded subheadings (defined by capital letters "A," "B," etc.). I coded for the type of argument (defined in chapter 2) and the total number of arguments presented in the case. Data sources: Litigant and *amicus* briefs on file at Washington University in St. Louis, Missouri.

Oral Argument Transcripts

I content analyzed the questions the justices ask during oral arguments to determine the types of information that they want. Again, I coded for types of arguments and for how many different arguments the justices raise. The coding is based on each question asked; therefore every question is considered a different argument. Specific rules I followed:

- Code all questions raised by the Court during oral arguments.

- Include, and count as separate questions, all repeat questions.

- Exclude incomplete sentences such as "Are we . . ." (unless you can discern what the question is asking—e.g., if the justice begins to ask about a precedent-setting case and is then interrupted by the attorney).

- Exclude any single-word responses such as "Okay."

- Count as one question any question where the justice begins speaking, is interrupted by counsel, and then finishes his or her sentence.

- Count as separate questions when counsel responds and the justice reiterates or restates the original question.

- Do not code retorts such as, "I think not."

- Do not count questions concerning issues such as, "Where is that in the brief?"

- Questions may be double coded. That is, a question may seek information about policy but also ask about what Congress thinks in this situation. This question would be coded as both a policy question and one about external actors (see Epstein and Knight 1998a for double coding rules).

Specific instructions for coding sheets:

- Write out each question verbatim.

- Write out who asked the questions (if you can determine who asked it).

- Mark the type of question (code 1–6 from coding scheme in chapter 2).

- If a comment involves more than one type, code for each issue type.

- Mark to whom the questioned was asked (appellant/petitioner, appellee/respondent).

- Count the total number of questions asked by the Court for each side and for the case as a whole.

- Code for whether the question raises a new issue (that is not found in the written briefs), or whether it focuses on an issue from a litigant or *amicus* brief.

Data sources: Oral argument transcripts on file at Washington University in St. Louis, Missouri.

Conference and Opinion Writing Process

Conference

I coded the conference notes of Justices Brennan, Powell, and Douglas, and characterized the remarks of each justice using specific issues. Specifically, I coded each sentence in the conference notes for each justice and counted the number of sentences that reference issues from the oral argument transcripts. If a justice's comments involved more than one type of argument (e.g., policy and constitutional issues) then I counted it as both types. I noted whether issues from the oral arguments were newly raised during these proceedings, or whether they were first raised in the briefs. Finally, I cross-checked with each of the other justices' notes to determine whether, for example, Brennan and Powell both noted that Justice White made a particular point. If so, I only coded it as one point. Otherwise I coded it as a separate point.

Data sources: Conference notes of Justices William J. Brennan and William O. Douglas, Library of Congress; Justice Lewis F. Powell Jr., Washington and Lee University School of Law.

Court Memoranda

I coded all intra-Court memoranda—either sent to the entire Court or sent privately between two or more justices. Specifically, I coded each sentence in the memoranda and counted the number of sentences that referenced issues from the oral argument transcripts. If a justice's comments involved more than one type of argument (e.g., policy and constitutional issues) then I counted it as both types. I coded for the specific issue type and for whether the issue was

newly raised at the oral arguments, or was first brought up in the briefs. I excluded opinion drafts and memoranda that did not explicitly address an issue in the case (e.g., memoranda that simply said "Please join me.")
Data source: Case files of Justice Lewis F. Powell Jr., Washington and Lee University School of Law.

Court Opinions

I coded the syllabus of each case to ascertain the principal arguments set out in the majority opinion. The principal arguments are defined as the numbered arguments in the syllabus. If these arguments were too vague (e.g., "Law X violates the First Amendment") then I coded the subarguments, defined by letters (e.g., "A," "B," etc.). Specific instructions used on the coding sheets:

- Code for issue type as with briefs, oral arguments, conference notes, and memoranda.
- Code for whether issues in the syllabi come from the briefs only, the briefs and the oral arguments, or from the oral arguments only.

Data source: Syllabi found at http://www.findlaw.com.

Appendix 2:
Data Reliability

I conducted reliability analysis on the dependent variable for each of the empirical chapters. For chapters 2 and 4 and the first half of chapter 5 I conducted the analysis on a random sample of eight cases (constituting 11 percent of the total cases in the sample). A research assistant used the coding scheme outlined in chapter 2 and the coding rules outlined in Appendix 1 to code the briefs, oral argument transcripts, and conference notes. A meeting was held with the coders to allow them to ask clarifying questions about the coding scheme. A meeting was also held after the coding was complete to rectify any disagreement.

I employed a similar procedure to determine the reliability of the dependent variable in chapter 3 (Justice Powell's citations to his colleagues' oral argument questions and comments) and the dependent variable used in the second half of chapter 5 (the number of citations to oral arguments in the Court's majority opinions). However, in chapter 3 a research assistant recoded the entire sample of cases ($N = 128$). In chapter 5, a research assistant recoded approximately 10 percent of the cases ($N = 500$).

With the coding complete, I compared my codes with those completed by the independent coders for each dependent variable. Specifically, I calculated interagreement scores that yielded a kappa statistic for each category. Generally, a kappa of 1 indicates perfect agreement, and a kappa of 0 indicates agreement due to chance (Landis and Koch 1977; see also Cohen 1960). Landis and Koch (1977) argue that any kappa above .80 indicates almost perfect agreement, while those above .60 show substantial agreement among the coders.

The results of the kappa tests suggest that my data are quite reliable. This is shown in table A.1. All of the categories reach statistically significant kappas, and for six of the categories the rate of agreement is well over 75 percent. The final category, the conference notes, yields a significant kappa but falls just short of what Landis and Koch suggest is an acceptable level of agreement (kappa = .59). However, because these are the most subjective data I employ, this is still a respectable level. Additionally, even for the conference notes the rate of agreement was almost seven times greater than what one would expect by chance. In short, the data used throughout the book may be subjective, but they are highly reliable.

Table A.1
Data Reliability

Category	Agreement (%)	Expected Agreement (%)	Kappa	Z
Litigant and *amicus* briefs	88.99	37.72	.82	10.3***
Oral argument transcripts	78.65	18.96	.74	43.18***
Powell's references to colleagues' preferences (chapter 3)	88.37	24.24	.85	18.25***
Conference notes	62.50	9.38	.59	5.58***
Opinion syllabi	91.18	33.56	.87	8.34***
Citations to oral arguments in majority opinions	98.40	70.44	.94	26.21***
Citations unique to oral arguments in majority opinions	98.20	78.50	.92	23.13***

* Significant at .10; ** significant at .05; *** significant at .001

Appendix 3:
Example of Justice Powell's
Oral Argument Notes from Chapter 3

Porter, Deputy Atty Gen of Calif

1. ~~&~~ Sexual conduct regulated is ~~e~~ not protected by 1st Amend.

2. If regarded as "speech", the "obscenity" standard does not apply to the regulation of liquor.

3. Fed. Ct. may not enjoin otherwise valid reg. because of alleged improper motive

The Rules go only to "sexually oriented acts"

(J. Stewart) emphasized that the Regulations relate to ~~a~~ sale of ~~ssss~~ liquor' — not to regulation of 1st Amend. Rts.

La Rue - 112

Hertzberg (for appellee)

~~Ess conflict~~

(Stewart) ~~so~~ asked whether State could prohibit sale of liquor in a book store? Hertzberg answered "NO". But he admitted State may prohibit sale near a school or a church. (He could not defend this distinction)

Stewart pressed this point.

139

Hertzberg admitted State has
exceptional power over ~~~~
public sale of liquor.

He argued that State could
not regulate ~~sale~~ or forbid the
of liquor in the lobby or allies
of the theatre

State could however forbid the
sale at the gate of an ~~zoo~~ foundry
(Responding to Q by (Marshall)).

La Rue (3)

Hertzberg (cont).

Scholty (for appellee also).
St. cannot prohibit serving of
whites & blacks in same bar because
of probability of fights.

(J. Stewart emphasized that
the regulation is of liquor & where
it is sold. It is not a regulation
of 1st amend. or R.ts.)

Notes

Chapter 1. Introduction

1. Indeed, as the public learned when the Court released the audiotapes of *Bush v. Gore* (2000), the justices clearly gather information during oral arguments as they ask the attorneys many intricate legal questions. To hear this and many other oral arguments navigate to www.oyez.org/oyez/frontpage.

2. Segal and Spaeth also argue that because they found no references to the phrase "oral arguments" in Justice Powell's docket sheets, these proceedings are not pertinent for the justices. In contrast to this assertion, chapter 4 of this book demonstrates that even though the justices may not use the words "oral arguments" in conference discussions, they nonetheless discuss issues from these proceedings, including many issues that entered the record of a case for the first time during oral arguments. Additionally, I demonstrate that these issues are discussed in intra-Court memoranda sent between chambers during the opinion-writing process.

3. This view is also perpetuated by the plethora of judicial process texts that include extensive discussions of each aspect of the Court's decision-making process, but include only cursory sections about oral arguments. These sections, if included at all, simply explain the process of these proceedings without discussing the role they may play for the Court (see e.g., O'Brien 2000; Smith 1993; Carp and Stidham 1996).

4. Interestingly, these scholars have not yet not empirically tested this claim.

5. By ignoring these proceedings, I mean that judicial process scholars generally address oral arguments by simply recounting the process and procedures of oral arguments, while ignoring how these proceedings might affect the Court's decisions (see e.g., Carp and Stidham 1996; but see Baum 2001).

6. Although the trial of this case concerned libel law, the case before the Supreme Court dealt only with the issue of discovery during the trial and the implications of the protective order on the paper's First Amendment rights.

7. They are right to note (Epstein and Knight 1995, 22) that this number would probably be higher had they also had access to more than just Brennan and

Marshall's papers for this study. Indeed, if they could have seen the private memos sent or received by all of the justices who were on the Court during the time period of their sample, their hypothesis may have been supported with even stronger evidence.

8. Other scholars have provided evidence of strategic interaction at almost every stage of the Court's decision-making process, including during the agenda setting (*certiorari*) stage (Caldeira, Wright, and Zorn 1999), during oral arguments (Johnson 2001), and during conference discussions (Johnson, Spriggs, and Wahlbeck 2002).

9. Congress can also overturn constitutional decisions, but it is much harder because it takes a constitutional amendment to do so. The difficulty lies in the fact that it takes a two-thirds majority of both houses to pass an amendment, which must then be ratified by either three-fourths of the state legislatures or three-fourths of constitutional conventions in each state.

10. This particular battle did not end with the RFRA, however. Indeed, in *City of Boerne v. Flores* (1997), the Court ruled that Congress exceeded its authority by passing the RFRA. This meant that the justices effectively overruled the act, and reinstated *Smith* as the controlling precedent over religious freedom cases.

11. Segal (1997) takes issue with the notion that justices ever account for the preferences of Congress and argues that they overwhelmingly engage in rationally sincere behavior. While he makes a cogent argument about why justices may be rationally sincere, the balance of the evidence in the literature suggests otherwise (Epstein and Knight 1998a; Martin 1996, 1997; Maltzman, Spriggs, and Wahlbeck 2000).

12. The remainder of this section is taken from Johnson (2003), "The Supreme Court, the Solicitor General, and the Separation of Powers."

13. The exceptions clause in Article III of the Constitution gives Congress the power to alter the Court's appellate jurisdiction as it sees fit.

14. That a case must be justiciable also stems from the Article III requirement that the Court can only decide cases and controversies. For instance, cases cannot be moot (*DeFunis v Odegaard* 1974), but must also be ripe for review (*Longshoremen's Union v. Boyd* 1954).

15. This and the other Supreme Court rules can be found on the World Wide Web at http://www.law.cornell.edu/rules/supct/overview.html.

16. Note that these numbers do not include appendices or supplemental briefs. While the clerk of the Court will reject briefs with egregiously long appendices, the parties often double or triple the length of their briefs by adding them at the end.

17. A typical *amicus* case contains not 1, but 4.4 briefs from *amici curiae* (Epstein 1993). This means that on average the Court also has about 150 pages of arguments beyond those presented by the parties. Today, more than 75 percent of all cases decided with a full opinion include at least one amicus brief (Epstein et al. 1996, 647).

18. This could be the case for many reasons, but one pertinent example is the idea that justices may be sanctioned for deciding issues *sua sponte*; that is, if they decide on issues that are not part of the legal record (Epstein, Segal, and Johnson 1996).

19. Of course, as Hoekstra and Johnson (1996) point out, the justices can gather additional information in other ways. For instance, they may ask that the parties brief specific issues; they can solicit *amici curiae* to give them information; and they can ask for reargument. However, all of these means of obtaining information are rarely used. One may also argue that the justices can simply send their clerks out to conduct this sort of research, but given the increasing time and workload constraints facing the justices (Baum 2001), particularly as the number of *certiorari* petitions continues to increase, this information-gathering avenue is not opportune.

20. I use the pronouns her and him, as well as he and she, interchangeably throughout the manuscript.

21. Miller and Barron (1975) reach similar conclusions in their analysis of the oral arguments in *New York Times v. Sullivan* (1964).

22. Other studies have considered oral arguments. However, these have either followed tacks similar to Cohen and Benoit's by studying few cases (McFeeley and Ault 1979) or have focused on teaching future advocates how to prepare for oral arguments (see e.g., Engel 1981; Prettyman 1984; Shapiro 1984). Beyond these, journalistic accounts dominate the literature about oral arguments (Biskupic 1999; Galloway 1989; Savage 1997).

23. Note that there has been criticism of the process. The major problem justices have with oral argument is its frequent low quality. Chief Justice Burger summarizes this position: "The quality is far below what it could be" (in Stern, Gressman, and Shapiro 1993, 571). Further, Justice Powell was disappointed at the level of advocacy when he joined the bench. "I certainly had expected that there would be relatively few mediocre performances before the Court. I regret to say that performance has not measured up to my expectations" (in Stern, Gressman, and Shapiro 1993, 571).

24. In recent years, the audio transcripts have become available for over 300 cases at http://www.oyez.org/oyez/frontpage.

25. Although there is no indication of why the Court does not identify specific questioners, it is possible that the justices do so in an attempt to indicate that it is actually the Court asking the questions, rather than nine individuals who are doing so.

26. As noted above, the official transcripts of oral arguments do not indicate which justices ask which questions. Thus, these data only allow me to assess claims about aggregate Court behavior. To solve this problem, I take two tacks. First, I use Justice Powell's oral argument notes to discern if he utilizes theses proceedings in a manner similar to the Court as a whole. Second, I take a sample of cases from Kurland and Casper (1975) and assess how three other justices—Brennan, Stewart, and White—use oral arguments. Combining these data with Powell's notes gives me the ability to assess how a number of different justices, with disparate ideologies, utilize these proceedings to gather information.

Chapter 2. Oral Arguments as an Information-Gathering Tool

1. This introductory paragraph relies heavily on Epstein and Kobylka (1992) unless otherwise noted.

2. This exchange is taken from the transcript of *Roe* and can be found at http://www.oyez.org. Note that in about 2 percent of all cases the parties are asked to submit additional briefs to the Court and to reappear for a second oral argument. For an analysis of when cases are reargued, see Hoekstra and Johnson (1996, 2003).

3. The Court does take this tack in some cases. Indeed, Hoekstra and Johnson (1996) find that when asked to reargue a case, the justices often tell the parties what they should argue. More often than not, the parties respond accordingly. For an example see *Patterson v. McLean Credit Union* (1989).

4. This calculation does not account for the fact that some cases were scheduled for more than the one hour allotted for oral arguments under the rules governing the Burger Court (Stern, Gressman, and Shapiro 1993, 571–2). However, the fact remains that this is a significant number of questions even in a two-hour session.

5. As chapter 1 indicates, Congress and the executive branch have formal mechanisms to sanction the Court. Congress can try to overturn the Court's decisions, and the executive branch can withhold enforcement. The public may sanction the Court by simply refusing to follow the Court's decree. For instance, in *Santa Fe Independent School District v. Doe* (2000) the Court determined that school-sponsored prayers may not be broadcast over a public address system prior to a football game. Media accounts suggest that this decision has been disregarded by many school districts (see e.g., LRP Publications 2000a, 2000b).

6. In this example, O'Connor's question focuses on whether Congress historically has acted in a certain way. If justices are strategic, they should be more concerned with the preferences of the current Congress than with those of the enacting Congress (Epstein and Knight 1998a). However, the context of the question in this case indicates that O'Connor sought to determine what the current Congress would do in light of what past Congresses did with this area of the law.

7. Rule 14 stipulates that *certiorari* briefs must contain a statement of jurisdiction. Rule 24 stipulates that a similar statement must be made in the briefs on the merits.

8. Rule 34.2 states: "Every document exceeding five pages (other than a joint appendix), whether prepared under Rule 33.1 or Rule 33.2, shall contain a table of contents and a table of cited authorities (i.e., cases alphabetically arranged, constitutional provisions, statutes, treatises, and other materials) with references to the pages in the document where such authorities are cited."

9. Presumably this means the Court may not hear cases that do not meet certain threshold standards. For instance, a case must be live (*DeFunis v. Odegaard* 1974), the parties must have proper standing (*Flast v. Cohen* 1968), and the Court will not decide political questions (*Baker v. Carr* 1962).

10. Circumstances may change, as they did in *Craig v. Boren* (1976). In this case—concerning whether a state could allow women to buy beer when they turned eighteen, while men could not do so until they were twenty-one—the petitioner (Craig) turned twenty-one after the Court agreed to hear the case. Thus, it was possible that this case was moot—no more controversy existed because Craig could legally buy beer.

11. I operationalize "new" as meaning information that was not provided in the litigant or *amicus curiae* briefs. Of course, these may not be new issues per se because they may have been derived from a lower court opinion or from the Court's past decisions, but they are "new" issues for the case at hand. Thus, because they enter the record for the first time in the form of a question asked by a justice during oral arguments, I code them as "new."

12. The Inter-University Consortium for Political and Social Research initially provided these data, through Washington University in St. Louis. The cases were drawn from the Spaeth (2003) database with the following STATA commands: Keep if ANALU==1 or ANALU==.; keep if issue>=401 and if issue<=537; keep if term >=72 and term <=86; drop if Oral == ".". The resulting sample of cases is 389. From this I randomly selected 75 cases, or about 20 percent of the cases on which I conduct my analysis.

13. The analysis of these cases is conducted separately. The *N* for cases without *amici* is 45, and the *N* with *amici* is 30.

14. Briefs on the merits must follow the same rule as *certiorari* briefs explained in Supreme Court Rule 14.1(a). It reads: "A petition for a writ of certiorari shall contain . . . The questions presented for review, expressed concisely in relation to the circumstances of the case, without unnecessary detail. The questions should be short and should not be argumentative or repetitive . . ." The key problem with this method, given Rule 14, is that the questions presented section simply raises the general issues covered in a case and does not consider the specific legal arguments that may be made by the parties.

15. The only difference between my coding scheme and that used by Spriggs and Wahlbeck is that I use the main headings in the Argument section of the briefs' index rather than the headings in the body of the brief. Because these headings are the same, this poses no problems.

16. Remember that I could have also coded the arguments presented by the litigants, but because I am concerned with the information that justices want, as opposed to what counsel want them to have, I focus exclusively on information sought by the Court.

17. Recent technological innovations have now made this type of analysis possible. Indeed, for a sample of about 300 cases, the OYEZ Web site http://www.oyez.org/oyez/frontpage includes digital copies of the oral arguments, along with written transcripts that identify which justices ask which questions.

18. Justice Powell did not note every question he asked during oral arguments, and he did not make reference to every issue raised by the parties. Rather, he noted only about ten issues (on average) per case. Given that the Court itself raised eighty-eight questions per case (which does not include the issues raised by the parties), I assume that Powell wrote down only those arguments he believed were important. This may seem

like a leap of faith, but I believe it is a logical assumption given that the justices are goal oriented. Indeed, they should only be concerned with issues that will help them reach their goals or alternatively with how they can overcome issues that might impede their efforts (e.g., institutional barriers, a congressional override, etc.).

19. These cases are: *New York Times v. Sullivan* (1964), *Bell v. Maryland* (1964), *Heart of Atlanta Motel v. United States* (1964), *Ginzburg v. United States* (1966), *Miranda v. Arizona* (1966), *California v. Stewart* (1966), *Katzenbach v. Morgan* (1966), and *Webster v. Reproductive Health Services* (1989).

20. The justices are Brennan, White, and Stewart.

21. However, these justices do cross the ideological continuum on the Court. Powell is the relative conservative, White and Stewart moderates, and Brennan the liberal. So with these data I can make initial tentative claims about whether justices with different agendas and goals seek similar information during oral arguments.

22. A pilot study of a select few oral argument transcripts, combined with earlier research on legal argumentation before the Court, led me to create this finite set of categories. At first the coding scheme included nine different categories, but I determined that several could be combined. The final scheme includes six categories.

23. I do not expect the Court to spend a great deal of time discussing constitutional issues during oral arguments. If the justices do so, then this would be evidence against the strategic account of how the Court utilizes these proceedings. Indeed, I expect a strategic justice to be more concerned with questions about policy and external actors' preferences than with questions about constitutional doctrine.

24. Note that I may underestimate the use of precedent. Court rules specify that litigant briefs must list all relevant precedents at the start of the document (Supreme Court Rule 24.1(d)). However, I only code references to precedent that are invoked in the main argument section of the briefs. I do so because I want to capture only those cases that counsel believes are most important for their case rather than every case they cite in the hope that it may help them win.

25. The categories are not mutually exclusive, and double coding was utilized. Thus, an argument could be a constitutional issue and also a policy issue. This convention follows Epstein and Knight (1998a), and they provide examples of how one issue may be coded as two types. The reader should also note that this coding scheme is subjective but highly reliable. Indeed, intercoder reliability analysis produces highly significant kappas for each phase of the coding (see Cohen 1960; Landis and Koch 1977). This analysis can be found in appendix 2.

26. Epstein and Kobylka (1992) make a compelling argument that the bulk of the most important information the Court receives prior to the oral arguments comes from the litigant and *amicus curiae* briefs.

27. McGuire (1993a) does not specifically argue that the lawyers know the justices are policy oriented. However, he does suggest that those who argue before the Court are more inclined to deal with "legal abstractions and the policy implications of litigation" (70).

28. Note that all briefs, per Supreme Court rules, must state the facts of the case. Rule 24.1(g) says, "Briefs should include a concise statement of the case, setting out the facts material to the consideration of the questions presented, with appropriate references to the joint appendix." Like the coding of precedent, the data here only capture times when one of the main arguments forwarded by the parties involves a question of fact. For instance, in *Barnes v. United States* (1973), a case involving stolen mail and other property, the petitioner raised the issue, "Was the evidence sufficient to show the defendant had in his possession stolen mail which he knew was stolen?" This type of factual argument is included, while statements of simple who, what, or when are not.

29. Even when these categories are combined, the justices still ask more questions about policy (p = .001).

30. Hague ultimately won the case. The trial court concluded that Minnesota's choice-of-law rules required the application of Minnesota law and granted summary judgment for respondent. The Minnesota Supreme Court affirmed, and the U.S. Supreme Court affirmed this decision.

31. Five restrictions were codified by the city. These included: (1) all abortions after the first trimester must be performed in a hospital; (2) parental consent for all women under fifteen years of age seeking an abortion; (3) physicians must provide information about the procedure and the physical and emotional effects of having an abortion; (4) a twenty-four-hour waiting period before an abortion is performed; and (5) fetal remains must be disposed of in a humane manner.

32. Under the rational basis test, the city would only have to prove that it "had acted reasonably to achieve a legitimate government objective" (Epstein and Walker 1998b, 453). The opposite of the rational basis is that the government must prove that it has a compelling interest rather than simply a legitimate objective. Thus, a rational basis approach leads the Court to more often find in favor of the government regulation. For an analysis of typical standards used in abortion cases see Epstein and Walker (1998b, 462), where they delineate the strict scrutiny test, the undue burden test, and the rational basis test.

33. The compelling reasons were often limited to pregnancy or the birth of an illegitimate child.

34. A bar letter is meant to stop the recipient from entering the premises of a military installation without the express permission of the commanding officer.

35. Clearly the solicitor general would have some explicit knowledge of the government's position (Meinhold and Shull 1998; Deen, Ignagni, and Meernik 1998; Pacelle 2003). There may be some concern whether this is the case for a normal lawyer. However, in thoroughly researching a case, it is likely that counsel would generally have knowledge of what other relevant actors think about a case.

36. Scholars argue that justices seek this information because the Court's key power lies in the degree to which the public views it as a legitimate institution, and it has been documented that the Court responds to public preferences (see e.g., Stimson, MacKuen, and Erikson 1995; Jones and Hoekstra 1997). Scholars have also shown that

the justices care about the Court's legitimacy, and that they discuss these types of issues in their internal deliberation process (see e.g., Epstein and Knight 1995, 1998a). Additionally, evidence indicates that the public does respond to the Court's decisions (Franklin and Kosaki 1989; Johnson and Martin 1998).

37. See the discussion of *Seattle Times Co. v. Rhinehart* in chapter 1.

38. The data in my sample show that the parties do not raise nearly as many precedents as Knight and Epstein (1996). However, we collect our data differently. They use the list of cases that a brief cites, therefore capturing every single case listed in a brief. This follows Supreme Court Rule 24.1(c), which states: "If the brief exceeds five pages, a table of contents and a table of cited authorities" must be included. I code only the main arguments of a brief. Thus, I capture only precedents that the parties believe are important enough to merit specific reference in the argument section of the briefs.

39. There are two possible explanations, however, for why these issues are raised at all during oral arguments. First, a justice may raise them if she sincerely believes a case lacks jurisdiction or that a case is not justiciable. Second, and more realistically, a justice may raise these types of issues if she is worried that a decision may end up quite far from her preferred policy goals. In other words, she may raise them with the hope of getting a case dismissed as improvidently granted before it reaches conference.

40. If oral arguments meant little to the outcome of cases, then I would have expected different results than those I found. Indeed, I would have expected the Court to focus most of its attention on constitutional issues and questions of fact. The former would be a focus if the justices wanted the public to view the Court as highly legitimate, because by asking intricate constitutional questions, the justices would convey their legal expertise and their concern for the role of the Constitution in their decision-making process.

A similar explanation exists for factual issues. If the Court wanted to convey the sense that people can have their day in court before the Supreme Court, they would be much more inclined to ask an abundance of factual questions. As it is, the Court does ask quite a few of these questions, but again, they are clearly not a major focus. Overall, while the Court asks questions that do not fully support the strategic account of decision making, the justices do not raise them more often than those that will help them make policy close to their preferences. This suggests that there is some merit to the claim that the justices use oral arguments as a key information-gathering tool in their decision-making process.

41. This calculation excludes the factual questions asked by the Court, as there is no basis for arguing that these questions help the justices act strategically.

42. The difference between the number of questions asked about constitutional issues raised initially in a brief and those that are raised for the first time at oral arguments is not statistically significant ($p = .34$).

43. In these cases, difference of means tests show that the Court is significantly more likely to raise new issues about external actors' preferences than to address these issues if they are first raised by a litigant, an *amicus,* or by both a litigant and an *amicus.* The difference in each instance is significant at $p < .001$.

44. These differences are both highly significant as well.

45. McGuire (1993a, 1993b) argues that experienced attorneys do better before the Court than do attorneys with less experience. This may clearly affect the way in which oral arguments affect the Court. However, this hypothesis is not tested here. Instead, as I argue earlier in this chapter, as well as in chapter 1, I focus not on how attorneys use oral arguments to win their cases, but on how the justices use these proceedings to elicit the information that they want. Scholars who focus on oral arguments in the future may consider using McGuire's insights to test how attorneys with different levels of experience may use oral arguments to their advantage.

Chapter 3.   Oral Arguments and Coalition Formation

1. Page 8 of his oral arguments notes is the exact location where he notes Stewart's comments, while he notes White's comments on p. 7.

2. In the end, Powell actually joined the majority coalition, as did White. While Stewart agreed with most of the decision, he wrote a separate concurring opinion.

3. While this analysis is narrow because it is limited to one justice, it is easy to see how it applies to justices' behavior generally. Indeed, every justice must have information about how their colleagues want to act if they are to make decisions that will become good law and that also satisfy their own policy goals as closely as possible (Epstein and Knight 1998a). Thus, even though data exist to test only one justice's behavior, there is reason to believe that oral arguments serve the same function for most justices. Additional data may exist, but it is currently unobtainable. Indeed, other justices indicate that Chief Justice Burger kept notes during oral arguments (*This Honorable Court* 1988). However, his Court papers will not be available until 2024.

4. Justices also discuss a case as a Court during conference discussions. However, uncertainty has the potential to exist during and after these discussions (Johnson, Spriggs, and Wahlbeck 2002). The justices themselves are aware of this fact. As Justice Scalia put it, "In fact, to call our discussion of a case a conference is really something of a misnomer. It's much more a statement of views of each of the nine justices" (in O'Brien 2000, 207). Similarly, Chief Justice Rehnquist (2001, 257) argues, "The broad outlines emerge from the conference discussion, but often not the refinements." Thus, justices may know tentative votes, but not the type of arguments that each of their colleagues want to base their vote on after conference. Additionally, while *certiorari* votes may help justices predict case outcomes (Boucher and Segal 1995), they do not tell them anything about the specific policy choices that their colleagues want to make when deciding on the merits.

5. Note that cheap talk games are usually between two players. As a result, this analysis actually extends the logic of cheap talk theory to a game among nine actors.

6. Burt Neuborne is the Norton Pomeroy Professor of Law and Director of the Brennan Center for Justice at New York University.

7. Obviously, justices may want to learn about the preferences of those farthest away ideologically so they can determine what other coalitions may form. This tactic is unlikely to help justices coordinate through cheap talk, however, because it helps actors coordinate only when they share common interests (Farrell 1987; also see Morrow's 1994 discussion of party signals in Congress).

8. This sample includes the seventy-five cases used in chapters 2, 4, and 5, but includes an additional set of randomly selected cases to supplement the initial seventy-five. I collected additional data to ensure an adequate degree of variation, and a large enough N, for the dependent variable in the statistical models I employ in this chapter.

9. As note 3 suggests, this analysis focuses on one justice. However, given that game theory scholars argue that actors have information to make probability assessments about other actors' preferences but almost never empirically explore where this information comes from, this is a significant contribution to the literature.

10. As in chapter 2, policy statements are defined as those arguments that focus on legal principles the Court should adopt, courses of action the Court should take, or a justice's beliefs about the content of public policy (Epstein and Knight 1998a; Johnson 2001). See also table 2.1. A research assistant coded the full sample, and I recoded each case to test for reliability.

11. We achieved an 88.37 percent rate of agreement. This is quite high given the rate one would expect by chance (24.24 percent), and yields a kappa of 0.85 (p = .00), which suggests that these data are highly reliable (see Landis and Koch 1977). To correct the 12 percent error, we sat down and determined the proper way to code each of the discrepancies.

12. While a Poisson model is also an appropriate modeling choice for count outcomes, the data I employ do not lend themselves to this technique. Indeed, of the 854 valid observations (those that remain after missing values are taken into account), only 143 have nonzero outcomes. As a result, the variance of the dependent measure is .32, which is greater than its mean of .20. This means that the Poisson model would produce consistent but inefficient estimates as well as downwardly biased standard errors (Long 1997, 230). Thus, I use the negative binomial regression model (Long 1997; Greene 1997), which accounts for the overdispersion of zeros by allowing "the conditional variance of y to exceed its conditional mean" (Long 1997, 230). An argument could also be made that I should use a zero-inflated model. However, there is no justification for arguing that any of the zeros in the model are there permanently (Long 1997; Greene 1997). Except in the rarest of instances (e.g., Clarence Thomas), all of the justices speak during oral arguments. Therefore, all of them have a chance to have Powell take note of their comments or questions. As such, while there is an overdispersion of zeros, there is little reason to believe that the sample is truncated between zeros that are part of the count data and those that remain zeros permanently.

13. Note that I tested other operationalizations of this variable. First, I used a dummy variable to distinguish the liberal and conservative justices. Additionally, I distinguished between the liberal and conservative justices by multiplying the liberal justice's distances by −1. I did so to determine whether there is a difference, beyond Euclidean distances, in whose comments Powell is more likely to note. Using either of

these measures did not change the substantive findings below; Powell is simply more likely to note questions asked by conservative colleagues.

14. I use the votes of the justices rather than another measure (Segal and Cover's 1989 scores) because justices have information concerning how their colleagues voted on certain issues for the entire time they have sat on the bench. Thus, votes are the most appropriate instrument for measuring Court ideology here, because they really do give the justices a clear idea of where their colleagues may come down in specific cases.

15. The intuition here is that Powell may only assess, and therefore note, the arguments of new justices because he does not know their preferences as well as colleagues with whom he has worked for a number of years. This is akin to the literature on socialization, freshmen effects, and voting fluidity (Hagle 1993; Howard 1968; Maltzman and Wahlbeck 1996a). Note that I also tested the new justice variable by coding it as only the first term that Powell and each colleague sat together on the Court. Doing so yields similar results.

16. The argument is that there is a greater probability of Powell noting someone's questions if they ask more questions. This follows from sociological literature on power that individuals have over groups. For instance, Bales (1970) and Schubert (1988) argue that those who speak more often in groups are perceived as being more powerful. Thus, those who talk the most during oral arguments could be seen as those whose votes are the most important to procure. Because these data are only available through 1981, O'Connor is excluded from the model.

17. I use natural Courts because the seating arrangement during oral arguments stays the same until a new justice joins the Court. Thus, the three seating arrangements in the sample are as follows: 1972—LFP, TM, PS, WOD, WEB, WJB, BRW, HAB, WHR; 1976—WHR, HAB, BRW, WJB, WEB, PS, TM, LFP, JPS; 1981—JPS, LFP, TM, WJB, WEB, BRW, HAB, WHR, SOC.

18. This may have been particularly true for Powell. Indeed, there is some indication that, at least after 1980, he had hearing problems. This is evidenced by correspondence he had with doctors at the Mayo Clinic. In one letter, dated November 7, 1988, he told a doctor: "I have had a hearing aid for my left ear for about five years, that I only needed in groups or where there was background noise. A couple of years ago an aid for my right ear was also recommended by the audiologist at Bethesda. Although this aid has been changed a couple of times, it never has worked successfully" (Powell, 1988).

19. Note that the negative binomial model, rather than a Poisson, is the appropriate modeling choice. I determine this through a significance test of the alpha coefficient presented in table 3.3. As Long (1997, 237) notes, "a one-tailed test of H_o: $\alpha = 0$ can be used to test for overdispersion, since when α is zero the Negative Binomial reduces to a Poisson." The results demonstrate that α is greater than 0. Thus, the negative binomial is better able to capture this phenomenon than a Poisson model. Additionally, the highly significant Wald χ^2 test indicates that the negative binomial model is more appropriate than the Poisson.

20. Initially, note that there is little evidence of a relationship between how often Powell cites a colleague's oral argument comments and the propensity for them

to join the same conference coalition. Indeed, even though the model performs well as a whole, the only significant predictor of Powell joining the same conference coalition as a colleague is the ideological distance between them. This is not an unexpected finding, however. One need only consider Chief Justice Rehnquist's argument (see note 4 in this chapter) that conference does not allow justices to fully flesh out the issues, as well as O'Brien's (2000, 207) argument that there is no time during conference to fully discuss a case. Rather, justices simply note their positions and tentative votes, with little additional comment. Additionally, Maltzman, Spriggs, and Wahlbeck (2000, 7) point out that conference votes are nonbinding and therefore also resemble cheap talk. In other words, because conference discussions are limited in scope and because votes often change after these meetings (Maltzman and Wahlbeck 1996a), Powell may not have had time to use what he learned during oral arguments to persuade his colleagues to join his coalition during conference. Thus, any purchase from his information gathering is more likely to be revealed during the opinion-writing process.

21. This variable is coded from the reported votes in each case. Note that there had to be full agreement; if Powell concurred in part and dissented in part, while a colleague simply dissented, they are not coded as being in the same coalition.

22. This final probability only changes to 98 percent if the justice is ideologically closest to Powell (i.e., 2.5 percentage points away from Powell with seven citations to oral argument comments).

Chapter 4. Conference, Opinion Writing, and Oral Arguments

1. Epstein and Knight's coding scheme for conference statements can be found in figure 2.1 of their monograph (Epstein and Knight 1998a, 30).

2. Note that any support I find for my hypotheses will be quite conservative estimates of the Court's use of oral arguments. Indeed, recall that I do not code arguments raised by litigants, but rather only questions the justices ask. Thus, any supporting data may actually underestimate the extent of the justices' reliance on oral arguments.

3. Certainly some of the issues are raised by more than one justice. But, that several justices weigh in with their opinions on a specific argument indicates a general tendency to debate issues from oral arguments in some detail. This clearly supports my argument.

4. This table also suggests that the Court almost never discusses issues during conference that are found in neither the briefs nor the oral argument transcripts. This supports Epstein, Segal, and Johnson's (1996) argument that the justices adhere to a norm of not deciding issues *sua sponte*.

5. Epstein and Walker (1998b, 393) note the key facts of *Gertz*. In this case, a police officer was convicted of murder, and Elmer Gertz was retained by the victim's family to sue Welch. Robert Welch covered the story and published an article in *American Opinion* that claimed Gertz was a "Communist-fronter" and wanted to defame and

frame the police. Gertz sued for libel and claimed that the story was a lie, hurt his career, and was not of public interest.

6. Note that as in chapter 2, the justices do not only deal with Congress. Rather, the Court often relies on state or local executive agencies for enforcement. The justices also rely on lower court judges to apply and implement their decisions properly.

7. This is not a surprise, given that almost all of the questions about external actors during oral arguments originate in these proceedings (see table 2.4).

8. For this analysis I combine the cases with and without *amicus curiae* participation.

Chapter 5. Oral Arguments and Decisions on the Merits

1. I use the major arguments found in the syllabus of the opinions. As chapter 1 points out, this approach allows for a clear comparison of the main issues raised by the parties and *amici*, and follows the accepted means of coding Court decisions (see e.g., Epstein, Segal, and Johnson 1996; Spriggs and Wahlbeck 1997). Two caveats should be made about this approach. First, the Court does not write the syllabi; the reporter publishing the cases does so. This introduces an outside, potentially biased, source into the equation. However, because I am interested in the use of information from oral arguments in the main issues decided by the Court, this seems the best and most objective means by which to compare the arguments and the opinions. Second, I may be losing information by not analyzing the entire opinions. As Wasby et al. (1992) find, there are many explicit referencpes to oral arguments in the Court's opinions (many times in footnotes). I lose these references by focusing only on the syllabi. The point is that the results presented here probably underestimate the Court's use of information from oral arguments.

Note also that two of the cases, *Parker Seal Co. v. Cummins* (1976) and *Poelker v. Doe* (1977), had no majority opinion writers. The first was decided by an equally divided Court, and the second was a *per curiam* opinion. Thus, while these cases are used in the aggregate analysis, they are omitted from the individual-level analysis.

2. For a description of *Mink,* see chapter 2.

3. Of course, there are cases when Powell clearly found the oral arguments unhelpful for deciding a case. In *Barnes v. United States*, for example, he noted that the petitioner provided a "Poor Argument" (Powell oral argument notes in *Barnes,* March 20, 1975).

4. Only one case—*Parker Seal Co. v. Cummins* (1976)—has no references to any issue from oral arguments.

5. Note also that this table provides additional evidence that supports Epstein, Segal, and Johnson's (1996) finding that the Court follows the norm of not deciding issues *sua sponte*. Indeed, only 9 percent of all issues found in the sample syllabi refer to issues not found in the litigant briefs, *amicus* briefs, or in the oral argument transcripts.

6. For this analysis, I combine the cases with and without *amicus* participation because separating the two decreases the number of opinions written by each justice to such an extent that I would not be confident in the results.

7. Note that the totals in this table will be different from those in table 5.1 because I exclude the two cases where there is no majority opinion writer. Thus, there are only 308 total syllabus arguments as opposed to 312 in table 5.1, which includes the two cases without a signed opinion.

8. The reader should heed some of these findings with caution, as the total number of syllabus points is quite small for some of the justices. Still, the results as a whole are quite consistent and tell a compelling story. Additional data collection could only strengthen the pattern that emerges in this table.

9. The briefs do focus on the general argument of police power, but not on these two key issues.

10. See chapter 2 for a description of the facts in this case.

11. The syllabus is the summary of the entire opinion and is not necessarily binding law.

12. As explicated in chapter 2, the question was whether, when a person was presented with a bar letter stating that he could not come onto the base without permission, how much time must lapse before the letter was stale? In short, does a decision to ban a citizen from the base last forever, or must the letter be renewed periodically?

13. As noted in chapter 2, if the justices were really concerned with the preferences of Congress, they should ask about the preferences of the sitting Congress. However, combined with the inquiry about the government, it seems that the justices were trying to put together a picture of what the law should mean in light of the preferences of those currently in power. Thus, the argument can be made that combined, these questions help the justices gain a sense of how others may react to their decision.

14. The median is often assigned a case for this purpose, as is demonstrated by Chief Justice Burger's assignment to Justice Blackmun in *Roe v. Wade* (1973) (see Hoekstra and Johnson 2003).

15. This paragraph is drawn from Hoekstra and Johnson (2003).

16. While I code all opinions, including dissents and concurrences, the analysis is limited to the majority opinions. On this point, see note 1 in this chapter.

17. Obviously I do not count instances where the Court references oral arguments from another court, or oral arguments in past cases. Rather I only code explicit references to oral arguments in the case at hand.

18. Note that the test of citation to orally argued issues is quite conservative. That is, I only capture instances where the Court's opinions actually use the words "oral argument" to determine where the information originated. Thus, I most likely underestimate the number of references to information from these proceedings. Indeed, the justices may cite information from the oral arguments but not say that the information comes from these proceedings (see Johnson 2001 and chapters 2 through

4). As Wasby et al. (1992, 17) note, "At times the Court has not referred to oral argument in the *per curiam* but may well have used oral argument in reaching its result." Any results from this analysis therefore probably underestimate the extent to which the justices invoke these proceedings as they craft their substantive legal and policy decisions.

19.   Reliability analysis demonstrates that even though the coding scheme is subjective, it is highly reliable.

20.   The calculation measures the ideological dispersion of the coalition based on the total number of liberal votes in each of Spaeth's (1999, 2001) issue categories. It therefore measures the level of ideological heterogeneity of the coalition (see Maltzman, Spriggs, and Wahlbeck 2000).

21.   For this variable I compared each justice's conference votes with his final votes on the merits. As table 5.7 indicates, this variable ranges from 0 to 9.

22.   I rely on Spaeth's (2001a, 2001b) data to determine whether the author of the opinion changed after conference (I utilize the aut1st, aut2nd, and aut3rd variables). If an opinion has been reassigned the case is coded 1, and 0 otherwise.

23.   Note that the negative binomial model, rather than a Poisson, is the appropriate modeling choice for both models. I determine this through a significance test of the alpha coefficient presented in each table. As Long (1997, 237) notes, "a one-tailed test of H_o: $\alpha = 0$ can be used to test for overdispersion, since when α is zero the Negative Binomial reduces to a Poisson." The results demonstrate that α is significantly greater than 0 in both tables. Thus, the negative binomial is better able to capture these phenomena than a Poisson model. The Wald test leads me to a similar conclusion.

24.   Because I have clear predictions about the directionality of the independent variables, I use one-tailed tests. This follows Blalock (1979, 163) who explains, "Whenever direction has been predicted, one-tailed tests will be preferable."

References

Abraham, Henry J. 1993. Judicial Process: An Introductory Analysis. New York: Oxford University Press.

Ackerman, Bruce A. 1984. "The Storrs Lectures: Discovering the Constitution." *Yale Law Journal* 93: 1013–72.

America and the Courts. 1998. C-SPAN. February 28.

Bales, Robert F. 1970. *Personality and Interpersonal Behavior*. New York: Holt Rinehart, and Winston.

Baum, Lawrence. 1995a. *The Supreme Court*. 5th ed. Washington, D.C.: Congressional Quarterly Press.

Baum, Lawrence. 1995b. "Symposium on Oral Argument." *Law and Courts* 5: 4.

Baum, Lawrence. 1997. *The Puzzle of Judicial Behavior*. Ann Arbor: University of Michigan Press.

Baum, Lawrence. 2001. *The Supreme Court*. 7th ed. Washington, D.C.: Congressional Quarterly Press.

Benoit, William. 1989. "Attorney Argumentation and Supreme Court Opinions." *Argumentation and Advocacy* 26: 22–38.

Bickel, Alexander M. 1962. *The Least Dangerous Branch: The Supreme Court at the Bar of Politics*. New Haven: Yale University Press.

Biskupic, Joan. 1999. "Sparring with the Supreme Court Nine." *Washington Post* November 1: A25.

Biskupic, Joan. 2000. "Masters of the Hypothetical." *Washington Post* January 3: A17.

Black, Duncan. 1958. *The Theory of Committees and Elections*. London: Cambridge University Press.

Blalock, Hubert M., Jr. 1979. *Social Statistics*. 2nd Ed. New York: McGraw-Hill.

Bork, Robert H. 1990. *The Tempting of America*. New York: Free Press.

Boucher, Robert L., Jr., and Jeffrey A. Segal. 1995. "Supreme Court Justices as Strategic Decision Makers: Aggressive Grants and Defensive Denials on the Vinson
Court." *Journal of Politics* 57: 824–37.

Caldeira, Gregory A., and John R. Wright. 1988. "Organized Interests and Agenda Setting in the U.S. Supreme Court." *American Political Science Review* 82: 1109–27.

Caldeira, Gregory A., John R. Wright, and Christopher J.W. Zorn. 1999. "Sophisti-
cated Voting and Gate-Keeping in the Supreme Court." *Journal of Law, Economics,
and Organization* 15: 549–72.

Cameron, Charles. 1993. "New Avenues for Modeling Judicial Politics." Presented at
the Conference on Political Economy of Public Law, Rochester, N.Y.

Carp, Robert A., and Ronald Stidham. 1996. *Judicial Process in America*. 3rd Ed. Washington, D.C.: Congressional Quarterly Press.

Chemerinsky, Erwin. 1989. "The Supreme Court, 1988 Term—Foreword: The Vanish-
ing Constitution." *Harvard Law Review* 103: 43–104.

Cohen, Donald. 1978. "Judicial Predictability in United States Supreme Court Oral
Advocacy: Analysis of the Oral Argument in *TVA v. Hill*." *University of Puget Sound
Law Review* 2: 89–136.

Cohen, Jacob. 1960. "A Coefficient of Agreement for Nominal Scales." *Educational and
Psychological Measurement* 20: 37–46.

Cooper, Phillip J. 1995. *Battles on the Bench: Conflict Inside the Supreme Court*. Lawrence:
University Press of Kansas.

Crawford, Vincent P., and Joel Sobel. 1982. "Strategic Information Transmission."
Econometrica 50: 1431–51.

Cushman, Robert E. 1929. "Constitutional Law in 1927–28: The Constitutional Decisions of the Supreme Court of the United States in the October Term, 1927." *American Political Science Review* 23: 78–101.

Danelski, David. 1978. "The Influence of the Chief Justice in the Decisional Process of
the Supreme Court." Pp. 506–19 in *American Court Systems: Readings in Judicial
Process and Behavior*, edited by Sheldon Goldman and Austin Sarat. San Francisco:
W.H. Freeman.

Deen, Rebecca, Joseph Ignagni, and James Meernik. 1998. "Explaining Presidential
Support on the Supreme Court: Ideology, Politics, and the Law." Presented at the
annual meeting of the American Political Science Association, Boston.

Ducat, Craig R. 1996. *Constitutional Interpretation*. 6th Ed. Minneapolis: West Publishing Company.

Engel, Albert. 1981. "Oral Advocacy at the Appellate Level." *University of Toledo Law
Review* 12: 463–71.

Epstein, Lee. 1993. "Interest Group Litigation During the Rehnquist Court Era." *Journal of Law and Politics* 9: 639–717.

Epstein, Lee, and Jack Knight. 1995. "Documenting Strategic Interaction on the U.S. Supreme Court." Presented at the annual meeting of the American Political Science Association, Chicago.

Epstein, Lee, Valerie Hoekstra, Jeffrey A. Segal, and Harold J. Spaeth. 1998. "Do Political Preferences Change? A Longitudinal Study of U.S. Supreme Court Justices." *Journal of Politics* 60: 801–18.

Epstein, Lee, and Jack Knight. 1998a. *The Choices Justices Make*. Washington, D.C.: Congressional Quarterly Press.

Epstein, Lee, and Jack Knight. 1998b. "Mapping Out the Strategic Terrain: The Informational Role of Amici Curiae." Pp. 215–36 in: *Supreme Court Decision Making: New Institutional Perspectives*, edited by Howard Gillman and Cornell Clayton. Chicago: University of Chicago Press.

Epstein, Lee, and Joseph F. Kobylka. 1992. *The Supreme Court and Legal Change: Abortion and the Death Penalty*. Chapel Hill: University of North Carolina Press.

Epstein, Lee, and Carol Mershon. 1996. "Measuring Political Preferences." *American Journal of Political Science* 40: 261–94.

Epstein, Lee and Jeffrey A. Segal. 2000. "Measuring Issue Salience." *American Journal of Political Science* 44: 66–83.

Epstein, Lee, Jeffrey A. Segal, and Timothy Johnson. 1996. "The Claim of Issue Creation on the U.S. Supreme Court." *American Political Science Review* 90: 845–52.

Epstein, Lee, Jeffrey A. Segal, Harold J. Spaeth, and Thomas G. Walker. 1996. *The Supreme Court Compendium: Data, Decisions and Developments*. 2nd Ed. Washington, D.C.: Congressional Quarterly Press.

Epstein, Lee, and Thomas G. Walker. 1998a. *Constitutional Law for a Changing America: Institutional Powers and Constraints*. 3rd ed. Washington, D.C.: Congressional Quarterly Press.

Epstein, Lee, and Thomas G. Walker. 1998b. *Constitutional Law for a Changing America: Rights, Liberties, and Justice*. 3rd ed. Washington, D.C.: Congressional Quarterly Press.

Eskridge, William N., Jr. 1991a. "Reneging on History? Playing the Court/Congress/President Civil Rights Game." *California Law Review* 79: 613–84.

Eskridge, William N., Jr. 1991b. "Overriding Supreme Court Statutory Interpretation Decisions." *Yale Law Journal* 101: 331–417.

Farrell, Joseph. 1987. "Cheap Talk, Coordination, and Entry." *RAND Journal of Economics* 18: 34–9.

Farrell, Joseph, and Robert Gibbons. 1986. "Cheap Talk in Bargaining." Mimeo. Cambridge, Mass.: MIT.

Farrell, Joseph, and Garth Saloner. 1985. "Standardization, Compatibility, and Innovation." *RAND Journal of Economics* 16: 70–83.

Ferejohn, John, and Barry Weingast. 1992. "Limitation of Statutes: Strategic Statutory Interpretation." *Georgetown Law Review* 80: 565–87.

Frank, Jerome. 1949. *Law and the Modern Mind.* New York: Coward-McCann.

Franklin, Charles H., and Liane C. Kosaki. 1989. "Republican Schoolmaster: The U.S. Supreme Court, Public Opinion, and Abortion. *American Political Science Review* 83: 751–71.

Galanter, Mark. 1974. "Why the 'Haves' Come Out Ahead: Speculations on the Limits of Legal Change." *Law and Society Review* 9: 95–160.

Galloway, Russell. 1989. "Oral Argument in the Court." *Trial* 25: 78–84.

Gely, Rafael, and Pablo T. Spiller. 1990. "A Rational Choice Theory of Supreme Court Statutory Decisions with Applications to the *State Farm* and *Grove City* Cases." *Journal of Law, Economics, and Organization* 6: 263–300.

Gibbons, Robert. 1992. *Game Theory for Applied Economists.* Princeton, N.J.: Princeton University Press.

Greene, William H. 1997. *Econometric Analysis.* 3rd Ed. Upper Saddle River, N.J.: Prentice Hall.

Hagle, Timothy M. 1993. "'Freshman Effects' for Supreme Court Justices." *American Journal of Political Science* 37: 1142–57.

Harlan, John. 1955. "What Part Does the Oral Argument Play in the Conduct of an Appeal?" *Cornell Law Quarterly* 41: 6–11.

Hensley, Thomas R., Christopher E. Smith, and Joyce A. Baugh. 1997. *The Changing Supreme Court: Constitutional Rights and Liberties.* Minneapolis: West Publishing.

Hoekstra, Valerie, and Timothy Johnson. 1996. "Arguing for the Sake of Arguing? The Influence of Legal Arguments on the Supreme Court's Decision Making Process." Presented at the annual meeting of the Southern Political Science Association, Atlanta. On file at the University of Minnesota.

Hoekstra, Valerie, and Timothy Johnson. 2003. "Delaying Justice: The Supreme Court's Decision to Hear Rearguments." *Political Research Quarterly* 56: 351–60.

Horwitz, Morton J. 1993. "The Supreme Court, 1992 Term—Foreword: The Constitution of Change: Legal Fundamentality without Fundamentalism." *Harvard Law Review* 107: 32–117.

Howard, J. Woodford Jr. 1968. "On the Fluidity of Judicial Choice." *American Political Science Review* 62: 43–56.

Huckfeldt, Robert, and John Sprague. 1995. *Citizens, Contexts, and Social Communication: Information and Influence in an Election Campaign.* Cambridge: Cambridge University Press.

Hughes, Charles Evans. 1928. *The Supreme Court of the United States; Its Foundation, Methods, and Achievements: An Interpretation.* New York: Columbia University Press.

Jackson, Robert H. 1951. "Advocacy before the Supreme Court: Suggestions for Effective Case Presentation." *American Bar Association Journal* 37: 801–4.

Johnson, Timothy R. 1995a. "Term Limits, Oral Arguments, and the Supreme Court." On file at the University of Minnesota.

Johnson, Timothy R. 1995b. "Legal Arguments and Supreme Court Decision Making: An Analysis of Early Obscenity Cases." Presented at the annual meeting of the Midwest Political Science Association, Chicago. On file at the University of Minnesota.

Johnson, Timothy R. 1996. "Bargaining, Strategy, and Supreme Court Decision Making." Presented at the annual meeting of the Midwest Political Science Association, Chicago. On file at the University of Minnesota.

Johnson, Timothy R. 2001. "Information, Oral Arguments, and Supreme Court Decision Making." *American Politics Research* 29: 331–51.

Johnson, Timothy R. 2003. "The Supreme Court, the Solicitor General, and the Separation of Powers." *American Politics Research*: 426–51.

Johnson, Timothy R., and Andrew D. Martin. 1998. "The Public's Conditional Response to Supreme Court Decisions." *American Political Science Review* 92: 299–309.

Johnson, Timothy R., James F. Spriggs II, and Paul J. Wahlbeck. 2002. "Passing as Strategic Voting on the U.S. Supreme Court." On file at the University of Minnesota.

Jones, Bradford, and Valerie Hoekstra. 1997. "Judicial Behavior in Political Context." Presented at the annual meeting of the American Political Science Association, Washington, D.C.

Kassop, Nancy. 1993. "From Arguments to Supreme Court Opinions in *Planned Parenthood v. Casey.*" *Political Science* 16: 53–8.

King, Gary. 1997. *A Solution to the Ecological Inference Problem: Reconstructing Individual Behavior from Aggregate Data.* Princeton, N.J.: Princeton University Press.

Knight, Jack. 1992. *Institutions and Social Conflict.* New York: Cambridge University Press.

Knight, Jack. 1994. "The Supreme Court and the Attitudinal Model Symposium." *Law and Courts* 4 1: 3–12.

Knight, Jack, and Lee Epstein. 1996. "The Norm of Stare Decisis." *American Journal of Political Science* 40: 1018–35.

Krehbiel, Keith. 1998. *Pivotal Politics: A Theory of U.S. Lawmaking.* Chicago: University of Chicago Press.

Kurland, Philip B., and Gerhard Casper. 1975. *Landmark Briefs and Arguments of the Supreme Court of the United States: Constitutional Law.* Vols. 58, 59, 60, 61, 63. Arlington, Va.: University Publications of America.

Landis, J. Richard, and Gary G. Koch. 1977. "The Measurement of Observer Agreement for Categorical Data." *Biometrics* 33: 159–74.

Lane, Charles. 2000. "Court Hears Arguments over Anti-Drug Tactics: Use of Roadblocks Is Weighed." *Washington Post* October 4: A19.

Lawrence, Susan E. 1990. *The Poor in Court: The Legal Services Program and Supreme Court Decision Making.* Princeton, N.J.: Princeton University Press.

Lazarus, Edward. 1999. *Closed Chambers: The Rise, Fall, and Future of the Modern Supreme Court.* New York: Penguin Press.

Levi, Edward H. 1949. *An Introduction to Legal Reasoning.* Chicago: University of Chicago Press.

Llewellyn, Karl. 1931. "Some Realism about Realism—Responding to Dean Pound." *Harvard Law Review* 44: 1222–37.

Long, J. Scott. 1997. *Regression Models for Categorical and Limited Dependent Variables.* Thousand Oaks, Calif.: Sage Publications.

LRP Publications. 2000a. "Sorting Out the Confusion about School Prayer." *Your School and the Law* 30 (October 10): 1.

LRP Publications. 2000b. "U.S. Supreme Court Declines to Review Graduation Prayer Appeal: Santa Fe Ruling Will Guide Future School Prayer Cases." *Your School and the Law* 30 (October 24): 1.

Lupia, Arthur, and Matthew McCubbins. 1998. *The Democratic Dilemma: Can Citizens Learn What They Really Need to Know?* Cambridge: Cambridge University Press.

Maltzman, Forrest, James F. Spriggs II, and Paul J. Wahlbeck. 2000. *Crafting Law on the Supreme Court: The Collegial Game.* New York: Cambridge University Press.

Maltzman, Forrest, and Paul J. Wahlbeck. 1996a. "Strategic Policy Considerations and Voting Fluidity on the Burger Court." *American Political Science* Review 90: 581–92.

Maltzman, Forrest, and Paul J. Wahlbeck. 1996b. "May It Please the Chief?: Opinion Assignments in the Rehnquist Court." *American Journal of Political Science* 40: 421–43.

Marks, Brian A. 1989. "A Model of Judicial Influence on Congressional Policymaking: *Grove City College v. Bell.*" Ph.D. dissertation, on file at Washington University, St. Louis.

Martin, Andrew. 1996. "The Separation of Powers and Strategic Decision Making on the Supreme Court: An Empirical Test." Presented at the Conference for the Scientific Study of Judicial Politics, St. Louis.

Martin, Andrew. 1997. "Designing Statistical Tests of Formal Theories: The Separation of Powers and the Supreme Court." Presented at the annual meeting of the Law and Society Association, St. Louis.

Martin, Andrew. 2001. "Congressional Decision Making and the Separation of Powers." *American Political Science Review* 95: 361–78.

McFeeley, Neil, and Richard Ault. 1979. "Supreme Court Oral Argument." *Jurimetrics Journal* 20: 52–83.

McGuire, Kevin T. 1993a. *The Supreme Court Bar: Legal Elites in the Washington Community.* Charlottesville, Va.: University Press of Virginia.

McGuire, Kevin T. 1993b. "Lawyers and the U.S. Supreme Court: The Washington Community and Legal Elites." *American Journal of Political Science* 37: 365–90.

McGuire, Kevin T., and Barbara Palmer. 1995. "Issue Fluidity on the U.S. Supreme Court." *American Political Science Review* 89: 691–702.

McGuire, Kevin T., and Barbara Palmer. 1996. "Issues, Agendas, and Decision Making on the Supreme Court." *American Political Science Review* 90: 853–65.

Meinhold, Stephen S., and Steven A. Shull. 1998. "Policy Congruence between the President and the Solicitor General." *Political Research Quarterly* 51: 527–38.

Miller, Arthur and Jerome Barron. 1975. "The Supreme Court, the Adversary System, and the Flow of Information to the Justices." *Virginia Law Review* 61: 1187–1245.

Moe, Terry M. 1982. "Regulatory Performance and Presidential Administration." *American Journal of Political Science* 26: 197–224.

Morrow, James D. 1994. *Game Theory for Political Scientists.* Princeton, N.J.: Princeton University Press.

Murphy, Walter F. 1964. *Elements of Judicial Strategy.* Chicago: University of Chicago Press.

Murphy, Walter F. 1966. "Courts as Small Groups." *Harvard Law Review* 79: 1565–72.

O'Brien, David M. 2000. *Storm Center: The Supreme Court in American Politics.* New York: W.W. Norton.

Pacelle, Richard. 2003. *Between Law and Politics: The Solicitor General and Civil Rights, Gender Discrimination, and Reproductive Rights.* College Station, TX: Texas A&M University Press.

Peterson, Merrill. 1987. *The Great Triumvirate: Webster, Clay and Calhoun.* New York: Oxford University Press.

Powell, Lewis F. 1988. "Letter to Dr. Douglas B. McGill; Personal Papers—Mayo Clinic." Papers of Lewis F. Powell Jr. Powell Archives, Washington and Lee University School of Law, Lexington, VA.

Prettyman, E. Barrett. 1984. "The Supreme Court's Use of Hypothetical Questions at Oral Argument." *Catholic University Law Review* 33: 555–91.

Pritchett, C. Herman. 1948. *The Roosevelt Court: A Study in Judicial Politics and Values, 1937–1947.* New York: Macmillan.

Rehnquist, William H. 1984. "Oral Advocacy: A Disappearing Art." *Mercer Law Review* 34: 1015–28.

Rehnquist, William H. 1986. "Oral Advocacy." *South Texas Law Review* 27: 289–303.

Rehnquist, William H. 1992. *Grand Inquests: The Historic Impeachments of Justice Samuel Chase and President Andrew Johnson.* New York: Morrow.

Rehnquist, William H. 2001. *The Supreme Court.* New York: Alfred A. Knopf.

Rohde, David W., and Harold J. Spaeth. 1976. *Supreme Court Decision Making.* San Francisco: W.H. Freeman.

Savage, David G. 1997. "Say the Right Thing." *American Bar Association Journal* 83 54–60.

Schubert, Glendon A. 1965. *The Judicial Mind: The Attitudes and Ideologies of Supreme Court Justices, 1946–1963.* Evanston, Ill.: Northwestern University Press.

Schubert, James N. 1988. "Age and Active-Passive Leadership Style." *American Political Science Review* 82: 763–72.

Schubert, James N., Steven Peterson, Glendon A. Schubert, and Stephen L. Wasby. 1992. "Observing Supreme Court Oral Argument: A Biosocial Approach." *Politics and Life Sciences* 11: 35–51.

Schwartz, Edward. 1997. "The Proliferation of Concurring Opinions on the U.S. Supreme Court: Politics Killed the Norm." Presented at the annual meeting of the American Law and Economics Association, Toronto.

Segal, Jeffrey A. 1997. "Separation-of-Powers Games in the Positive Theory of Congress and Courts." *American Political Science Review* 91: 28–44.

Segal, Jeffrey A., and Albert D. Cover. 1989. "Ideological Values and Votes of U.S. Supreme Court Justices." *American Political Science Review* 83: 557–65.

Segal, Jeffrey A., and Harold J. Spaeth. 1993. *The Supreme Court and the Attitudinal Model.* New York: Cambridge University Press.

Segal, Jeffrey A., and Harold J. Spaeth. 2002. *The Supreme Court and the Attitudinal Model Revisited.* New York: Cambridge University Press.

Seidman, Louis Michael. 1988. "Ambivalence and Accountability." *Southern California Law Review* 61: 1571–1600.

Shapiro, Stephen. 1984. "Oral Argument in the Supreme Court of the United States." *Catholic University Law Review* 33: 529–53.

Shapiro, Stephen. 1985. "Oral Argument in the Supreme Court: The Felt Necessities of the Time." Pp. 22–34 in *The Supreme Court Historical Society Yearbook.*

Slotnick, Elliot. 1978. "The Chief Justice and Self-Assignment of Majority Opinions." *Western Political Quarterly* 31: 219–25.

Smith, Christopher E. 1993. *Courts, Politics, and the Judicial Process.* Chicago: Nelson-Hall Press.

Smith, Craig R. 1989. *Defender of the Union: The Oratory of Daniel Webster.* New York: Greenwood Press.

Spaeth, Harold. 2001a. *Expanded United States Supreme Court Judicial Database, 1946–1968 Terms* [Computer file]. East Lansing, MI: Michigan State University, Program for Law and Judicial Politics [producer]. www.polisci.msu.edu/pljp.

Spaeth, Harold J. 2001b. *The Burger Court Judical Database, 1969–1985 Terms* [Computer file]. East lansing, MI: Michigan State University, Program for Law and Judicial Politics [producer]. www.polisci.msu.edu/pljp.

Spaeth, Harold J. 2003. *United States Supreme Court Judical Database, 1953–2001 Terms* [Computer file]. East Lansing, MI: Michigan State University, Program for Law and Judicial Politics [producer]. www.polisci.msu.edu/pljp.

Spriggs, James F., II, Forrest Maltzman, and Paul Wahlbeck. 1999. "Bargaining on the U.S. Supreme Court: Justices' Responses to Majority Opinion Drafts." *Journal of Politics* 61: 485–506.

Spriggs, James F., II, and Paul J. Wahlbeck. 1997. "Amicus Curiae and the Role of Information at the Supreme Court." *Political Research Quarterly* 50: 365–86.

Stern, Robert L., Eugene Gressman, and Stephen M. Shapiro. 1993. *Supreme Court Practice: For Practice in the Supreme Court of the United States*. 7th ed. Washington D.C.: Bureau of National Affairs.

Stimson, James A., Michael B. MacKuen, and Robert S. Erikson. 1995. "Dynamic Representation." *American Political Science Review* 89: 543–65.

This Honorable Court. 1988. Alexandria, Va: PBS Video.

Tushnet, Mark V. 1985. "Anti-Formalism in Recent Constitutional Theory." *Michigan Law Review* 83: 1502–44.

United States Supreme Court Reports on CD-ROM. 1996. Portland, Ore.: HoweData.

Wahlbeck, Paul J. 1998. "The Development of a Legal Rule: The Federal Common Law of Public Nuisance." *Law and Society Review* 32: 613–38.

Wahlbeck, Paul J., Forrest Maltzman, and James F. Spriggs II. 1996. "Strategic Choices and the Decision to Join the Majority Opinion." Presented at the Conference for the Scientific Study of Judicial Politics, St. Louis.

Wahlbeck, Paul J., James F. Spriggs II, and Forrest Maltzman. 1998. "Marshalling the Court: Bargaining and Accommodation on the United States Supreme Court." *American Journal of Political Science* 42: 294–315.

Wasby, Stephen L. 1993. *The Supreme Court in the Federal Judicial System*. 4th ed. Chicago: Nelson-Hall.

Wasby, Stephen L., Anthony A. D'Amato, and Rosemary Metrailer. 1976. "The Functions of Oral Argument in the U.S. Supreme Court." *Quarterly Journal of Speech* 62: 410–22.

Wasby, Stephen L., Anthony A. D'Amato, and Rosemary Metrailer. 1977. *Desegregation from Brown to Alexander: An Exploration of Court Strategies*. Carbondale: Southern Illinois University Press.

Wasby, Stephen L., Steven Peterson, James N. Schubert, and Glendon A. Schubert. 1992. "The Supreme Court's Use of Per Curium Dispositions: The Connection to Oral Argument." *Northern Illinois University Law Review* 13: 1–32.

White, Byron. 1982. "The Work of the Supreme Court: A Nuts and Bolts Description." *New York State Bar Journal* 54: 346–83.

Wolbrecht, Christina. 1994. "Separation of Powers, Constitutional Interpretation, and Free Exercise of Religion." Paper on file with the author at the University of Minnesota.

Woodward, Bob, and Scott Armstrong. 1979. *The Brethren*. New York: Simon and Schuster.

Cases Cited or in the Sample

Arcara v. Cloud Books Inc. 1986. 478 U.S. 697.

Allstate Insurance Co. v. Hague. 1981. 449 U.S. 302.

Baker v. Carr. 1962. 369 U.S. 186

Barnes v. United States. 1973. 412 U.S. 837.

Baxter v. Palmigiano. 1976. 425 U.S. 308.

Beal v. Doe. 1977. 432 U.S. 438.

Beauharnais v. Illinois. 1952. 343 U.S. 250

Bell v. Maryland. 1964. 378 U.S. 226.

Bender v. Williamsport Area School District. 1986. 475 U.S. 534.

Bigelow v. Virginia. 1975. 421 U.S. 809.

Bishop v. Wood. 1976. 426 U.S. 341.

Board of Education v. Allen. 1968. 392 U.S. 236.

Board of Education v. Pico. 1982. 457 U.S. 853

Braunfeld v. Brown. 1964. 366 U.S. 599.

Brown v. Board of Education. 1955. 349 U.S. 294.

Brown v. Glines. 1980. 444 U.S. 348.

Brown v. Hartlage. 1982. 456 U.S. 45.

Bush v. Gore. 2000. 531 U.S. 98.

California v. LaRue. 1972. 409 U.S. 109.

California v. Stewart. 1966. 384 U.S. 436.

Cantwell v. State of Connecticut. 1940. 310 U.S. 296.

Cantrell v. Forest City Publishing Co. 1974. 419 U.S. 245.

Chaplinsky v. State of New Hampshire. 1942. 315 U.S. 568.

Christian v. New York Department of Labor. 1974. 414 U.S. 614.

Chrysler Corporation v. Brown. 1979. 441 U.S. 281.

CIA v. Sims. 1985. 471 U.S. 159.

City of Akron v. Akron Center for Reproductive Health. 1983. 462 U.S. 416

City of Boerne v. Flores. 1997. 507 U.S. 521.

City of Madison Joint School District No. 8 v. Wisconsin Employment Relations Commission. 1976. 429 U.S. 167.

Columbia Broadcasting System v. Democratic National Committee. 1973. 412 U.S. 94.

Craig v. Boren. 1976. 429 U.S. 190.

Dartmouth College v. Woodward. 1819. 4 Wheat 518.

DeFunis v. Odegaard. 1974. 416 U.S. 312.

Eastland v. United States Service Fund. 1975. 421 U.S. 491.

Elrod v. Burns. 1976. 427 U.S. 347.

Employment Division, Department of Human Resources of Oregon v. Smith. 1990. 494 U.S. 872.

EPA v. Mink. 1973. 410 U.S. 73.

Erznoznik v. City of Jacksonville. 1975. 422 U.S. 205.

FDA v. Brown & Williamson Tobacco Corporation. 2000. 529 U.S. 120

First National Bank of Boston v. Bellotti. 1978. 435 U.S. 765.

Flast v. Cohen. 1968. 392 U.S. 83.

Forsham v. Harris. 1980. 445 U.S. 169.

Gagnon v. Scarpelli. 1973. 411 U.S. 778.

Georgia v. Evans. 1942. 316 U.S. 159.

Gertz v. Robert Welch Inc. 1974. 418 U.S. 323.

Givhan Western Line Consolidated School District. 1979. 439 U.S. 410.

Ginzburg v. United States. 1966. 383 U.S. 463.

Goss v. Lopez. 1975. 419 U.S. 565.

Greenholtz v. Nebraska Penal Inmates. 1979. 442 U.S. 1.

Heart of Atlanta Motel v. United States. 1964. 379 U.S. 241.

Heller v. New York. 1973. 413 U.S. 483.

Hortonville Joint School District No. 1 v. Hortonville Education Association. 1976. 426 U.S. 482.

Houchins v. KQED. 1978. 438 U.S. 1.

Hunt v. McNair. 1973. 413 U.S. 734.

Hynes v. Mayor of Oradell. 1976. 425 U.S. 610.

Immigration and Naturalization Service v. Chadha. 1983. 462 U.S. 919.

Jones v. Wolf. 1979. 443 U.S. 595.

Katzenbach v. Morgan. 1966. 384 U.S. 641.

Kelley v. Johnson. 1976. 425 U.S. 238.

Lemon v. Kurtzman. 1973. 411 U.S. 192.

Linmark Associates, Inc. v. Willingboro. 1977. 431 U.S. 85.

Longshoremen's Union v. Boyd. 1954. 347 U.S. 222.

Mapp v. Ohio. 1961. 367 U.S. 643.

Marbury v. Madison. 1803. 1 Cranch 137.

Marks v. United States. 1977. 430 U.S. 188.

Marshall v. United States. 1974. 414 U.S. 417.

Martin v. Ohio. 1987. 480 U.S. 228.

McGinnis v. Royster. 1973. 410 U.S. 263.

McKinney v. Alabama. 1976. 424 U.S. 669.

Memphis Light, Gas, and Water Division v. Craft. 1978. 436 U.S. 1.

Miami Herald Publishing Co. v. Tornillo. 1974. 418 U.S. 241.

Miller v. California. 1973. 413 U.S. 15.

Miranda v. Arizona. 1966. 384 U.S. 436.

Montayne v. Haymes. 1976. 427 U.S. 236.

New York v. Cathedral Academy. 1977. 434 U.S. 125.

New York Times v. Sullivan. 1964. 376 U.S. 254.

Paris Adult Theatre I v. Slaton. 1973. 413 U.S. 49.

Parker Seal Co. v. Cummins. 1976. 429 U.S. 104.

Patterson v. McLean Credit Union. 1989. 485 U.S. 617.

Pinkus d/b/a Roslyn News Co. v. United States. 1978. 436 U.S. 293.

Planned Parenthood of Central Missouri v. Danforth. 1976. 428 U.S. 52.

Planned Parenthood of Southeastern Pennsylvania v. Casey. 1992. 505 U.S. 833.

Poelker v. Doe. 1977. 432 U.S. 519.

Procunier v. Martinez. 1974. 416 U.S. 396.

Regan v. Taxation with Representation of Washington. 1983. 461 U.S. 540.

Roe v. Wade. 1973. 410 U.S. 113.

Rosenbloom v. Metromedia. 1971. 403 U.S. 29.

Santa Fe Independent School District v. Doe. 2000. 530 U.S. 290.

Saxbe v. Washington Post Co. 1974. 417 U.S. 843.

Seattle Times Co. v. Rhinehart. 1984. 467 U.S. 20.

Sherbert v. Verner. 1963. 374 U.S. 398.

Smith v. United States. 1977. 431 U.S. 291.

Tennessee v. Dunlop. 1976. 426 U.S. 312.

Tennessee Valley Authority v. Hill. 1978. 407 U.S. 153.

Turner v. Safley. 1987. 482 U.S. 78.

United States v. Nixon. 1974. 418 U.S. 683.

United States Postal Service v. Greenburgh Civic Associations. 1981. 453 U.S. 114.

United States v. 12 200-Foot Reels of Film. 1973. 413 U.S. 123.

United States v. Albertini. 1985. 472 U.S. 675.

United States v. Cherokee Nation of Oklahoma. 1987. 480 U.S. 700.

United States v. Weber Aircraft Corp. 1984. 465 U.S. 792.

Village of Schaumberg v. Citizens for a Better Environment. 1980. 444 U.S. 620.

Vlandis v. Kline. 1973. 412 U.S. 441.

Walz v. Tax Commission of the City of New York. 1970. 397 U.S. 664.

Ward v. Illinois. 1977. 431 U.S. 767.

Webster v. Reproductive Health Services. 1989. 492 U.S. 490.

Whalen v. Roe. 1977. 429 U.S. 589.

Widmar v. Vincent. 1981. 454 U.S. 263.

Withrow v. Larkin. 1975. 421 U.S. 35.

Wolman v. Essex. 1977. 433 U.S. 229.

Wooley v. Maynard. 1977. 430 U.S. 705.

World-Wide Volkswagen Corp. v. Woodson. 1980. 444 U.S. 286.

Zacchini v. Scripps Howard Broadcasting Co. 1977. 433 U.S. 562.

Index